# The Cultural Heritage of
# ARABS,
# ISLAM,
# AND the
# MIDDLE
# EAST

THE CULTURAL HERITAGE OF

# ARABS,
# ISLAM,
# AND THE
# MIDDLE
# EAST

WILLIAM G. BAKER

BROWN BOOKS PUBLISHING GROUP
DALLAS, TEXAS

For information, please contact
Brown Books Publishing Group
16200 North Dallas Parkway, Suite 170
Dallas, Texas 75248
www.brownbooks.com
972-381-0009

ISBN 0-9729578-0-4
LCCN 2003103303
First Printing, 2003

# Dedication

I dedicate this book to the memory of my first best friend and teacher of all things important and good in life, my older brother, Bronson Thomas Baker.

Arabs, Islam, and the Middle East

# CONTENTS

# Acknowledgments

I could not have acquired and internalized the material for this book had I not been raised from infancy through my teen years in the Arab culture. For this advantage I thank my father and mother, Dr. Dwight and Emma Baker, for having the wisdom and farsightedness to allow my brothers, sister, and me to spend the first years of our formal education in an all-Arabic school in the Palestinian city of Nazareth. Although this early education came at a small cost as we moved back and forth every five years between the Arab curriculum of Nazareth and the American curriculum of the United States, the linguistic and cultural advantages I gained by being immersed in the Arab culture in my youth allowed me to grow up with a foot in both the Arab and American cultures. No amount of adult formal education or money could buy the richness and multicultural awareness I acquired by growing up and remaining bicultural and trilingual. I also thank the members of my family, Carol, my wife, and Brent, Scott, and Holly, my children, for their support and constructive suggestions while writing the book.

My thanks and gratitude go to the Brown Books Publishing Group, especially Milli Brown, Kathryn Grant, and Alyson Alexander for their tireless efforts in guiding me through the publishing process.

I would like to single out one special person, Ms. Alexine Burke of Baylor University, for her genuine interest in my early manuscript. Her professional suggestions, corrections, and editing made this book the more readable product it is today. Thank you, Alexine, for your confidence in the significance of my work and for helping me bring to reality my first published book.

# FOREWORD

Few terms in Arabic are as important for the Westerner to know as *waseet*. A connotatively rich word, the word can mean agent, broker, intercessor, or mediator, depending on context. He is the individual who can mediate between feuding parties, settle business deals, and effect critical social arrangements. Throughout the Middle East, the role is as important as it is historically grounded. My colleague, Professor William Baker, a former military analyst who has served throughout the Middle East, is a *waseet*. Raised in the Middle East and educated in the United States, Bill's ability to navigate between the two cultures is simply unmatched. Whether teaching Arabic to gifted undergraduates in a liberal arts college or sitting with Palestinians to drink their coffee and share stories; whether lecturing on conflict in the Middle East or building an informal rapprochement with IDF border guards; Bill negotiates cultural difficulties with extraordinary aplomb. I know, for Bill has been my *waseet*, and I have seen firsthand his giftedness in building cultural bridges.

If I were to read any one book before traveling to the Middle East or doing business with those of that culture, this would be it. It is as authoritative as it is informative and entertaining. In a word, this text is the essential testimony of a *waseet*, the written wisdom of a true mediator between an East and a West that so need to rediscover the possibilities of friendship and peace.

—Jerry M. (Mark) Long, Ph.D.
Director, Middle East Studies
Baylor University

# The Arab World
## (Northwest Africa)

# The Arab World

## (East Africa and the Middle East)

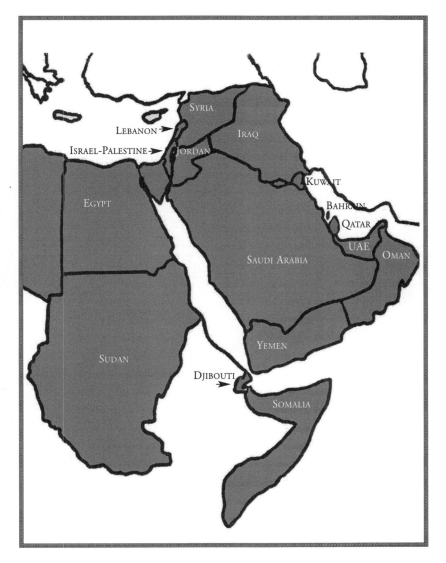

# INTRODUCTION

**M**y purpose for writing this book is to give the Westerner, especially the American, insight, knowledge, and understanding when dealing with Arabs, who live in a culture very different from that of the West. Westerners are not only underinformed about Arabs, but are generally ignorant of Arab contributions to the West and to the world in general. Some of these contributions are in the fields of science, mathematics, astronomy, architecture, and medicine. The world, especially the West, is also uninformed and misinformed about Arab culture, customs, mores, habits, turn-ons, and turn-offs. This lack of information can be critical when traveling in the Arab world and disastrous when attempting to do business from a Western focus in the Middle Eastern setting.

Please note the spellings of some Arabic names and words are different here than what you read in the newspapers and other Western texts. I have purposely spelled them so that the Westerner can better pronounce the words and names more closely to the Arabic sound.

This book is intended for anyone who wants or needs to understand the Middle East and its cultural and historical roots. In addition to providing information on the Arab world's historical, religious, and social connectivity, this book provides the Western reader with cultural dos and don'ts which become critical when traveling or doing business in the Arab Middle East. Those who would benefit the most from this book are first, businessmen and women who work with Middle Eastern markets; second, government and military officials assigned to the Middle East and who work with Middle Eastern issues; third, any undergraduate or graduate student of the Middle East undertaking a curriculum in Middle Eastern Studies; fourth, individuals who want a better understanding of Arabs and their very different culture; and fifth, anyone traveling in the Middle East who desires insight into this unique region we call the Arab world.

I wonder how many potential friendships were never given a chance to get past the introduction because of an uninformed Westerner's innocent gesture which was misinterpreted as insulting by an Arab; or by a Westerner's stereotyping an Arab because his clothing appeared "primitive" or his looks suspicious. I wonder how many business deals never had a chance to succeed because neither potential partner understood the basic elements of the other's culture in order to approach negotiations on familiar grounds.

This book is intended to be as much a guide for Westerners trying to understand Arabs, Muslims, and Middle Easterners, as it is for Arabs, Muslims, and Middle Easterners who need to know that Western approaches to them are often innocent and naïve, arising from a position of ignorance and a lack of Arab cultural awareness. Arab readers need to keep in mind that what appears obvious and second nature to them, the Arabs, is often foreign, and at times bizarre, to Westerners. In the same manner, some Western customs seem to lack respect and fall short of Arab standards of decency and morality. All readers should come to understand that the sword of cultural misunderstanding has two edges and can cut both ways. Just as one group is never completely right nor completely wrong when it comes to cultural variety, it takes both sides to show reason and tolerance of the other if there is to be understanding and cooperation.

Old Arab customs and mores are giving way to new ones, many influenced by the West. With instant communication and transcontinental travel as accessible and common as they are, not only the Middle East, but also the whole world, is changing. How the Middle East will look in the next fifty to one hundred years is anyone's guess. No doubt it will adopt some new Western ways, as it already has, but it will also certainly retain much of its cultural Arabesque which has distinguished it for centuries and so characterizes it today.

Having lived in the Middle East for more than twenty-three years with one foot in the American culture and the other foot in the Arab culture has given me the perspective, insight, and the privilege to accurately share with the reader my understanding and appreciation for Arabs in their native environment. By understanding Arab cultural mores and sensitivities, the Western student of the Middle East can avoid misrepresenting himself when interacting with Arabs. Although my intent is never to ridicule, belittle, assume, or intimate a higher moral, ethical, or cultural ground for one side against another, I do not shirk from calling things as I have seen and experienced them firsthand. If at times it is perceived by the reader that a specific cultural perspective appears more legitimate or "correct" than another, then such a conclusion is a result of the reader's cultural bias and perspective. If either the Arab or American reader is left with the impression that at times I appear to condemn or minimize one cultural perspective on a given point, it is because of my ability to lean on one cultural foot at a time, alternating between Arab and Western cultures in order to present an issue as it might appear through the other culture's eyes.

I drew extensively for this book from having been raised in the Palestinian-Arab community of Israel for seventeen years from 1950 to 1967. I also drew professionally and culturally on my extensive travels and assignments throughout the Middle East for twenty-nine years in both my military and civilian professions, totaling a combined regional experience of nearly fifty years. During this time I lived, worked, and traveled extensively among the Arabic and Hebrew-speaking inhabitants of Israel, and the Arabic-speaking, and Arabic cultural countries of Morocco, Tunisia, Egypt, Lebanon, Syria, Jordan, Saudi Arabia, Bahrain, Qatar, the West Bank (of the Jordan River), and the Gaza Strip (Palestine).

This book addresses the Arab cultural nations and treats them as parts of the pan-Arab cultural whole. Each Arab nation-state is part of the cultural pattern which comprises the complete Arab world. What we often casually refer to as the "Arab culture" or the "pan-Arab Nation" was, in reality, prior to Muslim Arab conquest and occupation, numerous distinct peoples and cultures, each with its unique history, heritage, religion, and traditions. These formerly distinct individual cultures have been blended over thirteen centuries of Arab rule, Arab cultural influences, the Muslim religion, and the Arabic language. This blend can accurately and confidently be referred to today as a culturally connected people with shared mores, customs, values, language, and for the most part, the same religion, who collectively identify themselves as Arabs.

# One

# Arab Identity

### Roots and History

In the preface, I wrote of having lived and traveled in "Arabic cultural countries," not simply in Arab countries. I make this distinction because most Arab inhabitants of Arab countries are not true Arabs, racially or ethnically. The only racially pure Arabs are the original native inhabitants of the Arabian Peninsula. Over the millennia, other ethnic groups from Africa and South Asia have mixed with the indigenous Arab population so that even today in the "home of the Arabs" there is much racial diversity. An Arab today is simply defined by the Arab League of Nations as anyone who speaks Arabic, has lived in an Arab country, and identifies with the Arab culture. With world travel as quick and accessible as it is, and with second and third generation Arabs living outside the Middle East or outside Arabic cultural countries, even this broad definition needs to be revised and updated to account for the increasing diversity. According to the Arab League's definition, although I was born an American to American parents of European descent with hundreds of years of American roots, going back to Scotland, Ireland, and England, I qualify as an Arab. How? I lived in a Palestinian-Arab cultural environment from the age of eleven months until eighteen years; I certainly identified with the Arab culture during this time because everyone in my life, except my parents, were cultural Arabs; and I grew up speaking Arabic natively. The Arabic language and the Arabic culture were so much a part of who I was that I was taught to read and write English as a foreign language by Arab teachers. Arabic was my de facto "mother tongue," even though my mother was not an Arab. I was so much stronger in Arabic than in English that my brothers and sister and I spoke Arabic at home; not with my parents, of course, for they were the foreigners.

As many Arab cultural scholars have thoroughly documented, although all Arab countries today have their own distinct histories, they all share a common Arab tradition imposed on their ancestors by Islamic armies in the seventh century. As these armies conquered countries of the Middle East, North Africa, Eastern and Western Europe, and Southwest Asia, they brought with them their religion (Islam), the Arabic language, and the Arabic culture. These three elements (the Arabic language, the Muslim religion, and the Arabic culture) were native only to the Arabian Peninsula until the Islamic conquest of what we know today as the Arab or Muslim world. In the wake of the Islamic military conquests of the seventh century, most inhabitants of these previously non-Arab countries eventually converted to Islam. Over generations of Arab occupation and rule, the descendants of these conquered people not only adopted the religion of their Arab rulers (Islam), they also became saturated with the Arabic language and culture. Today, these countries' previous cultural identities, that is, their culture as a unique people with their own language and traditions before the Arab conquest and occupation of their lands, are almost completely forgotten and lost. Some examples of these previously distinct cultures and people are the Phoenicians (today's Lebanese), Egyptians, Syrians, Libyans, Moroccans, and Palestinians. It does not take a cultural anthropologist to look at a Lebanese Arab today, side by side with a Saudi Peninsular Arab, to determine that they do not have the same ancestors or that they are not one and the same people ethnically, yet today we call them all Arabs because they call themselves Arabs. Original Phoenicians probably looked more like today's Greeks, Turks, or Syrians. Today's Lebanese have much eastern Mediterranean and European DNA mixed into their gene pool, thanks to conquering Greeks, Romans, and crusaders, as well as to many other racial contributors, because of Lebanon's fortunate (or unfortunate) crossroads geographical location.

Occupying Arab armies ruled portions of Spain for almost eight hundred years. If it were not for the deliberate efforts of the Spaniards to rid Spain of its Arab influences, known as the "*Reconquista*" (reconquest), much of Spain might still be speaking Arabic today and identifying with the Arab culture. Likewise, as many Middle Eastern scholars have pointed out, if it were not for Charles Martel, who defeated and stopped Arab-Islamic advance into western Europe at the Battle of Tours in France in 732 A.D., much, if not all, of Europe might be speaking Arabic and facing Makkah (Mecca) five times a day, as is the custom today in most of the countries conquered by Arab-Islamic armies. Had Arabism dominated European culture, it would not be too far-fetched to conclude that all countries subsequently colonized by European explorers four centuries later might well be speaking Arabic today, following the teachings of Muhammad, and identifying with the desert culture of the Arabs. This is put in perspective and becomes significant when we consider all the colonies of Great Britain, Spain, Portugal, and Holland in North, Central, and South America, Africa, India, and the Far East.

Much of what is known today as Spanish architecture has its roots in Arabic arches, courtyards, and balconies. The *Reconquista* notwithstanding, Spain and the Spanish language are still full of Arabic influences. A few common examples include: *vaca* (cow) from the Arabic *bakara*, *toro* (bull) from the Arabic *tor*, and *jarro* (jar) from the Arabic *jarrah*. Many Spanish proper names, such as the famous American baseball player Alomar, are derived from the Arabic *al-Omar. Al* is the Arabic definite article "the," and *Omar* is a common Arabic name, hence, Alomar, or "the *Omar.*" Names of places, such as *Elalambra* in Spain, come from the Spanish definite article *el* followed by the Arabic definite article, *al,* and *Hamra,* Arabic for "red" or "red one," hence, Arabic *al-Hamra* or "The Red One," because of the red color of the stones in the building. The Spaniards, obviously unknowingly, added the Spanish definite article *el* to the Arabic definite article *al* which made the word possess a redundant double definite article, *el-al,* or "the-the."

Most Westerners probably have never thought of how Gibraltar received its name. Gibraltar is Arabic for "*Jabal Tariq,*" or "mountain of *Tariq,*" named after the Moorish general who conquered and occupied it in the year 710 A.D. Spanish speakers call Gibraltar *Jebraltar,* the earlier corruption of the Arabic *Jabal Tariq.*

Many English words that start with the letters al (the Arabic definite article), especially scientific words, have Arabic roots. Words such as alchemy, algebra, alcohol, almanac, azimuth, nadir, and magazine, all come to the West from Arabic and the Arab age of enlightenment from the ninth through the twelfth centuries. During this period Arab scientists, mathematicians, navigators, astronomers, philosophers, architects, and doctors were preserving the works of the Greeks and adding to the world's scientific knowledge while Europe slumbered and stagnated in its Dark Ages. Undoubtedly, the West and the rest of the world today owe much to the early Arab scientists and scholars who contributed to and hastened Europe's Renaissance and the world's technological base, resulting in the Industrial Revolution and therefore placed the world in the technological position it is in today.

## A CULTURAL AND ETHNIC BASE

Today when we speak of the Arabic culture, we are talking of the common cord of identity that exists throughout the Arab world, or perhaps more accurately, the Arabic speaking world, with which all modern Arabs identify. Some of the more significant elements of this cultural cord are language, music, food, and to a greater degree, religion. There are also many elements to this cord of common identity, such as shared humor, common values, accepted norms of right and wrong, norms of public and private behavior, rites of marriage, and leadership selection, to name a few. All these are shared to a great degree across the Arab world, making it possible today to speak with confidence of a common pan-Arab culture. This pan-Arab cultural commonality affords an Arab residing in one Arab country little to no cultural adjustment when traveling to and dealing with Arabs from other Arab countries. By contrast, Westerners traveling to and from two Western countries would certainly have many cultural differences, beginning with a major obstacle, dissimilar languages. Even between two English speaking countries, such as the United States and England, there may be more cultural differences than between most Arab countries.

The reader should feel confident when dealing with people from any Arab country, whether they are Libyans, Egyptians, Syrians, Lebanese, Iraqis, or Qataris, that the cultural norms and conventions are more or less uniform in all these countries, with some regional adjustments and minor exceptions. For example, the mores and customs of North African Arabs (Moroccans, Algerians, Tunisians, and Libyans) may be somewhat different from those in the Levant (Lebanon, Syria, Palestine, and Jordan), or from the Arabian Gulf and Arabian Peninsula region (Kuwait, Bahrain, Qatar, United Arab Emirates, Oman, Saudi Arabia, and Yemen). If the Westerner applies the cultural characteristics identified in the next chapters when dealing with Arabs, he can feel confident that these characteristics will be universally applicable and understood throughout the Arab world.

Having defined modern Arabs, we now have a better understanding of who they are. Yet many people, especially

Americans who should know better because of their long association with the Arab world, often show amazing ignorance about who is and who is not an Arab. Therefore, a list of who is and who is not an Arab (and who is not an Arab but is often mistaken for one) is essential. The inhabitants of the following countries consider themselves to be Arabs: Algeria, Bahrain, Egypt, Iraq, Jordan, Kuwait, Lebanon, Libya, Morocco, Oman, Palestine,* Qatar, Saudi Arabia, Syria, Tunisia, the United Arab Emirates (UAE), and Yemen. Five other countries, Comoros, Djibouti, Somalia, the Sudan, and Mauritania, are also members of the twenty-two nation Arab League of Nations, or simply the Arab League (Eritrea is pending). Four of these (Djibouti, Somalia, Sudan, and Mauritania) are black African countries whose inhabitants speak Arabic and are largely Muslim, but who have retained some of their pre-Arab African culture. It is important to remember that all these countries identify themselves as Arab countries even though they may not be ethnically Arabs. Because their ancestors were conquered by Arabs more than thirteen centuries ago, the only culture they have to identify with today is that of their long-time occupier, the Arabs. In addition to identifying themselves with the Arab culture, all the inhabitants of these countries today speak Arabic and are largely Muslim.

Much confusion surrounds the following countries, which are largely Muslim by religion, but not Arab linguistically, ethnically, or culturally: Turkey, Iran, Pakistan, Afghanistan, and any other country ending with the "stan" suffix. Turkey and Iran are most commonly mistaken as being Arab. Turks are racially a Turkik-Asia Minor mix. Iranians are

---

*Although there is no internationally recognized country known as Palestine at the time of this writing (Fall 2002), Arab inhabitants of Israel, Palestine, and exiled Palestinian-Arabs are culturally and linguistically Arabs and for the most part Muslims.

racially a mix of Persian, Iranian, and other groups. Neither Turks nor Iranians speak, read, or write Arabic as their national language. Turks speak Turkish, of Turkik origin, written today in a Latin alphabet, and Iranians speak Farsi, an Indo-European language, which is written in the Persian-Arabic script. I am not sure which people seem more offended when confused for the other: Turks and Iranians when confused for Arabs, or the other way around. Refer to an Iranian or a Turk as an Arab, and see the reaction: quick denial and instant correction. From the confused, innocent, and uninformed Westerner's perspective, the objection seems bizarre and even humorous, but it is never taken lightly by the "offended" ethnic party.

The reader should have by now a good understanding of who Arabs are, who they are not, their perceptions of themselves, and their identity within the Arab world and the Arab community. The next chapter will focus on Arab cultural values and identify aspects of the Arab social character.

Arabs, Islam, and the Middle East

# Two

# Social Character

## A Sense of Identity

Arabs have developed an elaborate system of identifying themselves and others within Arab society as to their social class, rank, and position within the family, clan, or tribe. This system of identification undoubtedly has its roots in the early desert culture's need to quickly know whether a person being spoken to is a friend or a foe. In a desert environment with scarce resources (water, grazing land, women, personal wealth, and livestock), one is naturally suspicious of the intentions of strangers, their pedigree, family, clan, and tribal affiliation. In such an environment one needs to quickly establish with whom he is dealing. Therefore, a verbal social identification system which quickly identifies a person by tribe or clan is helpful in determining whether a person is a friend or a foe.

To facilitate this quick identification, Arabs have developed a system to identify a person's position in society which is built into each person's name. For example, if a man's name is *Omar*, and he is a father, he is given the social title of *Abu* (father) following his name. If his oldest son's name is *Ali*, the man's social name would be *Omar Abu Ali* (*Boo Ali* in North Africa) meaning "*Omar*, father of *Ali*." If this man's father's first name is *Muhammad*, he would also need to be identified as the son of *Muhammad*. Arabic for son, or "son of" is *Ibn* (sometimes *Bin*). This man's name would now identify him as *Omar*, father of *Ali*, son of *Muhammad*, and in Arabic would be stated as *Omar Abu Ali Bin Muhammad*. The person's paternal grandfather's name may also be included, following his father's name, in this case *Ibrahim*. The name is now *Omar Abu Ali Bin Muhammad Bin Ibrahim*. For further identification, if his family name is *al-Saud*, his name would be *Omar*, father of *Ali*, son of *Muhammad*, son of *Ibrahim* the Saud, and in Arabic would be stated as *Omar Abu Ali Bin Muhammad Bin Ibrahim al-Saud*. For final regional identification, if he is from the Saudi region of the Hijaz, his complete name could be *Omar*, father of *Ali*, son of *Muhammad*, son of *Ibrahim* the Saud of the Hijaz. In Arabic, his name would read *Omar Abu Ali Bin Muhammad Bin Ibrahim al-Saud al-Hijazi*. Add to this the title of sheikh, an honorary position of leadership and respect within Arab society which one is born into, and his name is now *Sheikh Omar Abu Ali Bin Muhammad Bin Ibrahim al-Saud al-Hijazi*.

Admittedly, this may be an extreme example, but it nevertheless shows what is possible. In reality, most Arabs carry only four names: their first name, their father's and grandfather's first names, and their family name. Therefore, our friend above would most likely only be known as *Omar Muhammad Ibrahim al-Saud*, which is quite manageable and comprehensible. However, to show that the above example is not too extreme, consider the Foreign Minister of Qatar in the early 2000s: *Sheikh Jassim Bin Hamad Bin Jassim Bin Jabir al Thani*. Translated into English, his name is Sheikh Jassim, son of Hamad, son of Jassim, son of Jabir from the Al Thani family. This is definitely a clear recitation of this man's lineage illustrating four generations.

In case the reader thinks this system is far-fetched, there are similar relationship identification markers in English names. In the early development of English names, someone who was the son of Jack was called Jack's son, later contracted and simplified to Jackson; son of William, Williamson; son of Eric,

Erickson; son of John, Johnson; and so on. In addition, one might be identified by his trade, such as Farmer, Goldsmith, Carpenter, Plumber, or Baker. As with some Arab names, some Western names are based on one's region, such as Scott for someone from Scotland, Frank for someone from France, "von der" and "de la," Dutch and Spanish, respectively, meaning "from the."

The Arab system of naming and social titling applies to women as well. As an example, consider an Arab woman named *Leila*. Arabic for mother is *Umm* (sometimes pronounced *Imm* in the Levant), and Arabic for daughter, or "daughter of," is *Bint*. The same rules apply as for the man above, and she would be known as *Sheikha Leila Imm Ali Bint Muhammad Bint Ibrahim al-Saud al-Hijazi*. In reality, as with males, females get a first name, followed by their father's and grandfather's first names, and their family name. So the above Arab woman's name would be *Leila Muhammad Ibrahim al-Saud*. Westerners may find it unusual that Arab women have male names as parts of their names. The reader will notice immediately the only part of an Arab woman's name which is female is her first name. This is because Arab society is male-oriented and patrilineal. In this regard Arabs differ from their Jewish cousins in that in Judaism, one's Jewish identity is determined by matrilineal heritage. The Jewish reasoning is that one always knows who the mother is, but one can never be 100 percent certain about the father (at least not until DNA identification came along).

As is obvious by now, in the Arab world a person's name is more than just a name, as it might be in the West. An Arab's name is his pedigree, which tells everyone exactly who he or she is within society.

This societal relationship identification does not apply only to fathers and mothers. As we have seen, it identifies sons and daughters, and it also identifies matrilineal and patrilineal aunts, uncles, and cousins. One's maternal aunt is known as *Khaalah*. Let's say one's maternal aunt's first name is *Widaad*. One would call her "my aunt," or *Khaalti*, (the *ti* suffix indicates possession), followed by her first name, *Widaad,* or *Khaalti Widaad,* "my maternal Aunt *Widaad.*" Using the same rules, but a different word for one's paternal aunt, *Ammah,* plus the *ti* possessive suffix, would be *Amiti.* Therefore, one would call a paternal Aunt *Widaad, Amiti Widaad.*

Maternal and paternal uncles also get distinct social titles and names. A maternal uncle is called a *Khaal,* plus a possessive *i* suffix; hence, one would call a maternal uncle *Khaali.* One's paternal uncle is called *Amm,* plus the possessive *i* suffix; hence, one would call a paternal uncle *Ammi.* Assuming the uncle's name is *Nabeel,* he would be called "my (maternal) Uncle Nabeel," or *Khaali Nabeel,* or *Ammi Nabeel* if he were a paternal uncle. This system of naming and social identification, which is strange to Westerners, is firmly in place and used every day across the entire Arab world from Morocco to the Arabian Gulf and beyond.

One last point of clarification regarding Arab names: Unlike their Western sisters, in some Arab communities women do not take their husband's last name when they marry. These women do not include their husband's last name as any part of their name after they get married, unlike women in the Spanish-speaking world who hyphenate their married and maiden names. From their specific Arab cultural perspective, to adopt their husband's family name and abandon their family birth name would take away their heritage. They would be giving up or losing part of their identity, in effect, erasing any trace of their correct lineage. It is sometimes confusing to Westerners to find an Arab husband and wife with two totally different last names, without sharing any part of either spouse's name. In a small way, these Arab women are more "liberated" than their Western sisters when it comes to maintaining their lineage, heritage, and identity. The concept of "your people shall be my people" as it applies to changing one's name is unimaginable in some Arab communities.

In conclusion, it is very important in Arab society to know one's kinship within a family, so much so that one is given a social title which identifies him or her specifically. This built-in verbal social identification system serves to establish one's position within the greater family, showing such important links as kinship, lineage, inheritance rites, and domicile, and gives one a sense of identification as part of the greater family. This social identifier also serves to mark one's position in the unwritten caste system, which will be discussed later in this chapter.

## GROUP RIGHTS, NOT INDIVIDUAL RIGHTS

In the West, people value privacy and the need to retreat to one's private space and world. The concept of privacy and the word "private," as Westerners understand them, do not have an equivalent or exact Arabic translation. There is no original Arabic word equivalent to the English word "private." Attempted Arabic definitions and translations are *shakhsi* (personal), or *khususi* (special or specific). None of these definitions capture the Western concept of intimate privacy to one's self, exclusive of all others.

It is probably no accident that the Arabic language and Arab society do not have a term or word for the concept of privacy. Arab society is not as concerned with the rights or interests of the individual as it is with the welfare and good of society as a whole, the group. This is, no doubt, a carry-over from desert culture survival requirements where little value and attention were placed on the needs and desires of the individual, but much value was given to the survival needs of the group. The wants of the individual are sacrificed for the needs of the many. As a result, in the Arab world, much less emphasis is given to legislation which upholds the individual rights that we hold so sacred in the West. For this reason, the West often finds itself at odds with Arab governments when it comes to identifying human rights and civil liberties, because both societies are using different standards. This priority given to the good of the group leads to consensus decision-making at all levels in Arab society.

## CONSENSUS AND INDIVIDUALISM

The emphasis on the good of the group rather than the interests of the individual is carried into Arab society's decision-making process at all levels, including government, where decision by consensus is the norm. Very rarely will one see an Arab country charge out on its own when considering regional issues without the consensus, or the approval, of the Arab community of nations. There are a few exceptions.

## EGYPT'S SEPARATE PEACE WITH ISRAEL

The most noteworthy exception in recent times was the separate peace treaty which Egypt's President Anwar Sadat made with Israel in the Camp David Accord of 1979. This issue affected the entire Arab world and its previously coordinated and agreed-upon position toward Israel. Prior to his trip to Jerusalem, President Sadat traveled to the Arab capitals of Damascus, Syria, and Amman, Jordan, to gain Arab consensus just to talk to the "enemy," Israel. When his first goal to gain Arab consensus on the issue failed, President Sadat continued with what he believed to be in Egypt's best interest, the chance to regain lost Egyptian territory and restore honor to the house of Egypt. To emphasize this point and show the consequences of breaking with traditional Arab consensus on such an important group issue (Egypt's separate peace treaty with Israel) first, caused Egypt to be cut off diplomatically and isolated from the Arab family of nations, and second and more importantly, cost President Anwar Sadat his life. It is impossible to overemphasize the weight and significance of consensus decision-making in the Arab world.

## IRAQ'S INVASION AND OCCUPATION OF KUWAIT

The other major break in consensus within the Arab family of nations in recent history was when Iraq's President Saddam Hussein defied Arab consensus and broke with his Arab brothers by invading and occupying Kuwait in 1990. This break caused him to not only be cut off and isolated economically and diplomatically from within the Arab family of nations, but also led to his defeat on the battlefield and its resulting shame.

Having established the importance of Arab consensus in decision-making, it seems somewhat contradictory to speak of individualism within the Arab world. Yet, Arab countries and their leaders like to think of themselves as individualists not tied to, led by, or following the dictates of any other country or its leader. On the surface, Arab heads of state put on the appearance of cordial cooperation, but underneath there is much individualism and disagreement.

## ARAB MUSIC

Perhaps the concept of Arab consensus and individualism can be illustrated through their music. In Arab music there is no harmony of parts; there is only one part, the melody. In Arab music, a singer always sings the single melody (individualism), or the entire group sings the same melody (consensus). A variation of this theme occurs when a lead singer is followed by a chorus of singers repeating and echoing the exact melody and words: individualism and consensus all at the same time. The Western notion of two, three, or four-part harmony is non-existent in Arab music. At this point, it might be tempting to interpolate that as goes Arab music, so go Arab cultural styles of leadership, individualism, and consensus.

## THE UNWRITTEN ARAB CASTE SYSTEM

Arabs are very careful with whom they associate socially. For this reason, they always ask one's name very deliberately up front, in an attempt to establish one's social position and family affiliation. The way they ask the question, either directly to the person at the first meeting or through a third party, is "From whose house are you?" Once one's heritage and social standing are established, the relationship can progress comfortably with everyone knowing how to proceed, either subservient or superior. Arabs are very careful not to associate socially with someone whom they think is below their socio-economic level. Arabs often tell professional Westerners living in Arab countries not to perform manual labor, such as washing their cars in public. Such actions are viewed as beneath the dignity of a college educated, professional person. Arabs will tell Westerners to hire someone of a lower socio-economic class to do that type of menial labor. The problem arises because Westerners, especially Americans, take pride in maintaining their cars and other possessions themselves. Definitely a difference in cultural perspectives.

## "WHERE ARE YOU FROM?"

A good example of Arabs attempting to establish pedigree, family affiliation, and social class occurred on three separate occasions when I met the Egyptian Defense Minister, the Emir of Qatar, and a Saudi prince. When I was first introduced to the first two men, as soon as I greeted them, they demanded, "Where are you from?" followed by "Who are you?" As an added point of confusion to both men, and all other Arabs whom I met for the first time, they were aware of my American national affiliation in the context of the introduction, but when I spoke Arabic to them without an American accent and with a native Arab accent, they immediately suspected I was an Arab, or a second or third generation Arab-American, and wanted to know where I was from and to which family, clan, or tribe I belonged. The instinctive desert cultural "friend or foe" inquiry automatically kicked in. The third example occurred when I met a prince in the Saudi royal family. He asked me if I were Lebanese even though I was introduced as an American. He was confused because my native Palestinian dialect was close to that of the Lebanese. As stated earlier, Arabs need to establish one's position in society immediately after an introduction in order to "protect" themselves and behave appropriately with the new acquaintance. Even though I insisted I was an American and even produced my American diplomatic passport, he refused to believe and accept me as "just" an American.

## SUSPICIOUS CURIOSITY

Because of their traditional desert cultural heritage, whether they live in the desert or in the city, Arabs generally tend to be suspiciously curious of strangers. In an anticipated meeting, much of the suspicion is not applicable. That is, if you as an American have an appointment to meet an Arab in his office and he knows of you and the purpose of the meeting before-hand, there is very little need for suspicion on his part and very little is exhibited. However, among Arabs, and between Arabs and Westerners or other strangers, whose ultimate motives are not readily known or accepted, Arabs feel there is reason for them to be suspicious and defensively cautious.

## NAZARETH, 1950

My family's move to the Middle East in June 1950 as Southern Baptist missionaries is a good example of Arab suspicion of strangers. My parents, with two very young boys, moved from Texas to the Palestinian-Arab city of Nazareth in Israel (Palestine). At first, all who met Dwight and Emma Baker in their newly adopted city of Nazareth were cordial but distant. To put the situation in perspective, Nazareth had come under Israeli rule only two years earlier. The new Israeli landlords were, for the most part, recent transplants from Europe. Four years earlier, the United States and its allies had resoundingly defeated Nazi fascism and Japanese colonialism. The United States was riding high as the single world super power, and its economy was creating great opportunities for its citizens after years of sacrifice during the war. Nazareth was a quiet, slowed-paced town with only four automobiles to its approximately thirty thousand inhabitants, and the Bakers owned one of the four. In this setting, we have Dwight and

Emma Baker, both about thirty years old, both with graduate degrees from United States universities, having left the real land of milk and honey to live in Nazareth because they cared about the salvation of the souls of the people of Nazareth. This scenario was unacceptable and therefore unbelievable to the war-weary, skeptical inhabitants of Nazareth. Add to this apprehension a dose of Arab desert cultural suspicion, and one can imagine the whispers among the people of Nazareth. As seen through the eyes of the local Nazareth Arab inhabitants, this young American couple claimed to care about the people of Nazareth, wanted to get to know them, wanted them to come to their home and wanted to visit them in their homes, wanted to learn their language, and were not asking for anything in return. Rumor had it that the Bakers were obviously CIA. It took my parents five full years before they were accepted for who they said they were, people who genuinely cared about the salvation of the inhabitants of Nazareth. Today, as I walk the streets of Nazareth, when I identify myself as the son of *Daktor Beikar,* I am honorably received with open arms and respect because my parents were ultimately accepted and respected.

## ASA AND HIS COUSIN

Another example of Arab suspicion of strangers occurred when I was visiting a Palestinian-Arab friend, Asa, in his home in Jaffa, Israel. Shortly into the visit, Asa's cousin walked into the room and I was introduced to him. I had just come from Syria and Lebanon and had crossed into Israel from Jordan across the Allenby Bridge. To put all this into context, the event took place prior to the Israeli-Jordanian peace agreement at a time when it was impossible for most people of the region, specifically Palestinian-Arabs, to travel to Jordan from Israel, much less from Syria to Israel via Jordan. It was also unlikely that many Arab inhabitants of Israel knew anyone who could undertake such travel. However, being in the United States military and working for the United States government with an official passport, I could and did accomplish this unimaginable feat. As I was talking about my recent travel, Asa began gesturing for me to change the subject. I understood his concern and changed the direction of the conversation to small talk. After his cousin left, I asked why the gesturing to stop talking in the presence of his cousin. Asa asked, "Do you know who my cousin is? Do you know who his friends are? Do you know who he talks to?" "No, of course not," I replied to all his questions. Then Asa said, "You can never be too certain to whom you are speaking, and it would be best if you said nothing of cross-border travel to a stranger." To put this in its greater perspective, at that time these were hostile borders between Israel and its neighbors, and security suspicions were compounded by natural Arab desert cultural suspicions.

This incident also points to Arab suspicions even among their own family members. Loyalty and trust among Arabs are extended first to their immediate family, followed by the extended family, which in the Arab world is much larger than that in the West, followed by the clan, tribe, and lastly, to this relatively new Western concept on the Arab scene, the nation. Remember, until not too long ago, Arabs lived in tribal areas not bounded by strictly defined borders in the Western sense. Most of the internationally recognized borders of the Middle East today were carved out and mandated by the West, namely Great Britain and France, following World War I and World War II.

## THE FRIEND OF MY FRIEND IS MY FRIEND

Having established Arabs' natural affinity for suspecting strangers, once Arabs accept someone as a friend there is nothing, unequivocally nothing, they would not do for their friend any time of the day or night, no exception. Arabs are world renowned for their overgenerosity and hospitality, especially by Western standards. I once was invited to the home of an Arab stranger as the guest of a friend of the house.

We arrived at midnight after a wedding feast and our hosts, whom I had never met before, woke up the local village shop-keeper to purchase food and drink to serve their friends and their friends' friend (me) because they had no provisions in their home. The purchase, I might add, was made with an IOU because our hosts were too poor to pay. This, I remind the reader, is from the same Palestinian-Arabs who held the missionary Bakers as suspect for five years. In all my travels throughout the world, I have never experienced anything that even comes a close second to the extent Arabs will go to host a friend or the friend of a friend.

## AL-UMMAH AL-ARABIYYAH

Following their immediate regional national identity as a separate people (Egyptians, Yemenis, Palestinians, and Moroccans), Arabs think of themselves as members of *al-Waton al-Arabi* or *al-Ummah al-Arabiyyah*, which closely translates to "The Arab Family of Nations," a concept which does not exist in the Western sense, but which encompasses all Arab nations across national boundaries in a confederation of one people linked by their common cultural, linguistic, and religious heritage. To Western students of the Arab world, the notion of pan-Arabism is dismissed as fantasy since Westerners see very little Arab agreement in any endeavor. It is an extreme irony that the only issue which unquestionably unifies Arabs is their hatred of the Jews (Israel). Western insight or shortsighted-ness notwithstanding, Arabs today identify themselves as members of this greater *Ummah al-Arabiyyah* connected to one another by a common cultural heritage, which includes a common code of social values. This pan-Arab common heritage was first brought to today's Arab world by Muslim Arab warriors over thirteen hundred years ago. The reality of the *Ummah al-Arabiyyah* will become evident throughout the next chapters as we continue to gain understanding of the Arab culture.

# Three

# Shame Versus Guilt

**A**rabs, more than Westerners, are motivated in their public and social interactions by outward appearances. What is more important to Arabs in their public and personal relationships is how things appear, and how others perceive them and that which they represent. Arabs could well have coined the Western phrase, "You only have one chance to make a first impression."

As a result of this emphasis on outward appearances, Arabs tailor their behavior, their actions, and all manner of activities according to how these actions or behaviors will be perceived by those who observe them. In the West, generally speaking, people are traditionally motivated in their actions with others based upon how things are and not so much on the appearance of how one wishes things to be perceived. This translates into marked differences in behavior between Arabs and Westerners. Westerners will do or not do something based upon their standards of right and wrong, and will usually behave in a certain way because they know they should, and because it is either right or wrong, based on culturally accepted absolutes. Arabs, on the other hand, are motivated much more by whether someone will see them act a certain way, and they will formulate their behavior based upon other people's perceptions and conclusions of their behavior.

For this reason, it is said that Arabs live in a shame-based society and Westerners live in a guilt-based society. There are, of course, many other people who live in a shame-based or guilt-based culture. Middle Easterners, Southwest Asians, and all Asians are generally shame-based societies. In reality, both Arab and Western societies act and react to some degree on the basis of both shame and guilt, although no society is completely shame-based or guilt-based. Westerners, many of whom come from a Judeo-Christian orientation, are instilled from an early age to live by a moral code of finite rights and wrongs. Westerners derive this concept from the Ten Commandments of the Old Testament (the Hebrew *Torah*), which constitute ten codes of conduct, dictating man's role with God and man's role with man. These commandments dictate strict codes of conduct and behavior to man ("Thou Shalt" and "Thou Shalt Not") and form the foundation of guilt-based behavior for Westerners. As a result, Westerners who adhere to this code live with an internal voice, or conscience, dictating that they should behave in a certain way because it is either the absolute right or the absolute wrong thing to do.

✳

## SANTA CLAUS

My best example of Westerners establishing an internal moral conscience occurred when I was about five years old. I asked my mother how Santa Claus could see me all the time and know if I was naughty or nice. She replied that Santa Claus had eyes in the corners of the ceiling of every room and could see my every move. I was afraid to undress in my room after that, thinking Santa would be watching me. My mother, the missionary, firmly instilled the guilt-based fear of God (Santa) into me at a very young age.

This is not to say that Arabs do not live by a high moral code of conduct; they do. The *Qur'an*, the Muslim Holy Book, is full of Islamic "Thou Shalts and Thou Shalt

Nots." The difference between the two cultures is often a determination by the impact of an Arab's actions on others. If performing a certain action would be harmful or cause someone to think negatively about the person performing the questionable act, then Arabs would think twice about doing so. Islam, and hence the Arab culture, is much more forgiving than are Christianity and Judaism. While there is the concept of finite good and evil and right and wrong in Islam, Islam also maintains the belief that all of one's actions, both good and evil, are recorded and will be evaluated on the Judgment Day. Islam recognizes the humanity and frailty of mankind and knows it is inevitable that humans will make mistakes in life. Western Judeo-Christian ethics assert that a person should strive to be faultless. Should a person fall short of perfection in the Judeo-Christian model, religion, and by social evolution, our culture places the heavy burden of guilt on the faltering individual. In Islam, on the Judgment Day, when all of one's actions are weighed, the good deeds should outweigh the bad deeds. If they do, one will receive his just reward accordingly. As a result, even if one makes mistakes in life, no single mistake or "sin" becomes a showstopper. No one mistake will necessarily determine if one goes to heaven or hell. Islam, and thus Arab culture, allows for deviations from the established norm without fear of not being able to recover. For this reason, when deciding whether or not to do something, a person in an Arab shame-based society will base his decision and action not only on whether it is absolutely morally right or wrong but also on whether anyone will witness that act and draw certain conclusions about the deed and the doer.

❁

## HONOR AND DISHONOR

If a person is influenced by whether someone sees him act in a certain way that would bring either honor or shame upon himself, then one is either honored or dishonored by his actions. Shame and dishonor, and pride and honor, take on a symbiotic relationship in Arab culture. The concept of a shame-based outlook has developed within Arab society a very strong motivation for doing that which will be seen by others as bringing honor to oneself and refraining from doing that which will be seen as bringing dishonor. This honor or dishonor may be extended to one's family, tribe, and society. Furthermore, people, leaders, and nations in the Arab world often feel the need to restore their honor when they perceive it to have been dishonored and/or perceived by others as having been dishonored. This reasoning is very similar to the Old Testament "eye for an eye and tooth for a tooth" concept of justice. This means if A has dishonored B, B may take revenge to avenge the dishonor, which alone will restore the honor. The best way to describe how a shame-based philosophy translates into everyday life is to provide the following examples.

## WEDDING FLASH

I once was invited to a Bedouin wedding by an Arab friend. Bedouins (more correctly Bedu) are Arab desert nomads who follow fertile grazing lands for their herds of camels, sheep, and goats. I asked my friend if it was permissible for me to take pictures of the wedding. He asked a family member of the wedding party, and the answer came back yes. Members of the bride's and groom's families were pleased to see me, a foreigner, interested in them enough to be taking pictures at their wedding. Unfortunately, I very quickly ran out of film. Many members of the wedding party continued to come to me asking me to take their picture, which would honor them. After all, I had taken pictures of their brothers, cousins, or friends, so I should equally honor them by taking their pictures as well. I explained my predicament to my friend who asked if my flash was still working. I said yes. My Arab friend suggested I continue to flash as though I were taking pictures, and no one would know or be offended. I protested that would be untrue (lying), to which my friend asked, "Will anyone ever know?" Thus, I continued to honor them by "taking their pictures" and did not dishonor them by refusing to take their pictures. There certainly was a lot of guilt within me, knowing I was deceiving those whose pictures I was not really taking, but there was no dishonor, and thus no shame, to the recipients of my actions. What guilt and/or shame existed was within me, the Westerner. It was not so important how things really were but how things appeared to others.

## ODOMETER SETTING

An Arab friend of mine had recently returned from the Czech Republic where he visited his son who was in medical school. I asked if he had been able to see some of the country while he was there. He responded that he had and related the following story to me. While in the Czech Republic he had rented a car for thirty days and toured the entire country. He was unhappy that the rental car company was going to charge him so much money for every kilometer he had driven. He declared, "They were going to fix me; so I fixed them instead." After driving the car to his son's apartment, he disconnected the odometer cable. He then drove the length and breadth of the country after which he reconnected the odometer cable a week before returning the rental car. According to his way of thinking, the rental car company was attempting to unfairly charge him for every kilometer, so he was justified in doing to them first that which they were attempting to do to him. My friend was proud of his accomplishment. There were no victims. He could walk with head raised because he was not taken (dishonored) by the rental car company's unfair treatment. More so, among his own, he was a hero because he gave the rental car company what he considered to be a dose of their own medicine.

## MUNKAR

Alcohol is forbidden in Islam; so much so that it is given the adjective *munkar*. *Munkar* simply means that which is to be refused, denied, forbidden, or taboo. My favorite definition of *munkar* (alcohol) identifies it as "moral filth and turpitude." Simply put, in Islam, alcohol is filthy and forbidden by the *Qur'an*. On one occasion I was assigned as the escort officer to a Saudi Arabian Air Force general who was visiting the United States Air Force Academy, where I taught Arabic. Before I had a chance to introduce myself to the visiting general, he had ordered a Coors Beer by name and was waiting for me in the lounge. I waited for the right moment to challenge his choice of beverage, all in good humor. When the beer arrived and he took the first sip, I walked up to him and said in native Arabic, "*Hada munkar, la*?" (This is *munkar*, no?) He immediately put down the beer with a look of the proverbial cat that swallowed the canary and with total confusion, as he saw me standing before him dressed in a United States Air Force uniform. What he saw was an American who seemed to have much insight into his culture and language, but what he heard was a fellow native Arab holding an incriminating eyewitness account of his consuming *munkar*, and he was very confused. His first reaction was to ask who I was. After he was more or less satisfied that I was not a fellow Muslim who observed him violating a religious taboo, he explained to me that alcohol was only *munkar* in Saudi Arabia. How convenient, I thought, God does not travel with one on business trips. That which is forbidden in one's home county is permissible if not witnessed by a fellow Muslim, and if no one is harmed. The general and I continued to talk, and it became evident that he was well educated and was very familiar with Christianity. He cited the New Testament reference to Jesus performing the miracle of turning water into wine at the wedding in the village of Cana in the Galilee region of northern Palestine. The general commented, "What a great way to start a religion. Your Messiah's first miracle was to serve you alcohol!"

## MIG SHOOTDOWN

On another occasion I came to know an Egyptian Air Force colonel while assigned as his escort officer in the United States. The colonel was attending the United States Air War College in Montgomery, Alabama. I asked him if there were Israeli officers in the school with him, and if so, how they got along. This was two years following the Israeli-Egyptian Camp David Peace Accord of 1979, which returned the Sinai Peninsula to Egypt in exchange for a peace treaty with Israel. The Egyptian colonel answered that there was an Israeli Air Force colonel in his class and even in his seminar group, and they were cordial but not overly friendly in the classroom since there were other Arab officers in the same seminar. Outside the seminar setting, he admitted, they had become good friends. Remember, it is all about appearances. The Egyptian Arab could not appear to be too friendly to the Israeli, his traditional enemy, in front of other Arabs, lest he appear to betray the Arab cause; that would be traitorous and dishonorable.

The Egyptian officer volunteered the following incident. When he first met the Israeli colonel, he, the Egyptian officer, saluted the Israeli officer and thanked him for an Israeli Air Force shoot-down some years earlier of five Egyptian MIG-21 fighter aircraft in a specific engagement. This confused both the Israeli colonel and me. He explained that until that fateful day when the Israeli Air Force shot down five Soviet-built fighter aircraft, Soviet Air Force pilots, tacticians, and trainers, who were in Egypt to equip and train the Egyptian Air Force, would constantly belittle the Egyptians and all Arabs, claiming that they were inferior in skill and intellect, as well as being inferior fighters and pilots. These were the reasons, the Russian trainers would tell the Egyptians, that the Israelis were constantly victorious over greater Arab numbers and superior Soviet equipment, training, and tactics. The Soviets would never acquiesce that it might have been inferior Russian equipment, training, and tactics which resulted in Israeli victories and Arab defeats. The Egyptian colonel then explained that he had saluted the Israeli colonel and thanked him for the shoot-down of the Egyptian MIGs over the Sinai Desert because, on that particular day, the Egyptian MIGs were piloted by five Soviet pilots, who, as it turned out, were inferior to the Israelis in skill and tactics. The Egyptian colonel said that was the proudest day of his life because on that day honor had been restored in the Egyptian and Arab camps and shame had been removed.

## EGYPT WON THE 1973 WAR

There is a monument in the city of Cairo, Egypt, to commemorate the Egyptian victory over Israel in the October 1973 Yom Kippur/Ramadan Arab-Israeli War. Arabs refer to this war as the Ramadan War because it began on the first day of the Islamic holy month of Ramadan, a month of fasting, intense prayer, and spiritual renewal. Israelis refer to the October conflict as the Yom Kippur War because it started on the highest holy day in Judaism, the Day of Atonement (Yom Kippur in Hebrew). Following initial successes by the Egyptian military in breaching Israeli defenses on the east bank of the Suez Canal, Israeli forces counter-crossed the Sinai Peninsula into Egypt and routed the Egyptian Third Army, encircling them and demanding Egyptian capitulation. To Israel and the West, since Israeli forces were ultimately the victors on the battlefield, militarily speaking, Israel is credited with having won the war. However, to Egypt the issue was much broader than battlefield success on the last day of the war. At this point, some background information is needed: In the June 1967 Six-Day War, Israel had captured all of the Sinai Peninsula from Egypt and had refused to return it until Egypt signed a formal peace treaty. Egypt, on the other hand, refused to sign a peace treaty with Israel until Israel first returned the Sinai. What we had was a classic Middle East standoff, which caused these traditional adversaries to be their own worst enemies for the sake of principle.

Ultimately, as a result of the Yom Kippur/ Ramadan War, Israel and Egypt eventually sat down at the bargaining table at Camp David, Maryland, brokered by United States President Jimmy Carter and signed a formal peace treaty. The treaty returned the Sinai Peninsula to Egypt in stages, in return for a formal peace treaty with Israel. So how, a Westerner might ask, did Egypt win the Ramadan War? Egyptians and Arabs both reason that had Egypt not dealt Israel a severe blow on the battlefield in the early days of the 1973 War (the war was quite costly to Israel in terms of lives and equipment lost), Israel would not have had the incentive to sit down at the peace table, subsequently agreeing to withdraw from the Sinai Peninsula, and Egypt would not have recovered the land it had lost to Israel. Egypt's loss of the Sinai Peninsula to Israel in 1967 was a source of severe damage to Egyptian pride and honor, resulting in shame to both Egypt and the *Ummah al-Arabiyyah* (the Arab Nation). The 1973 War resulted in the Camp David Accords which called for Israel to relinquish the Sinai Peninsula to Egypt. The return of this territory to the Egyptians was the undoing of their shame and the restoration of honor to the Egyptians and to the *Ummah al-Arabiyyah* (The Arab Nation) as well. Hence, as far as the Arabs were concerned, Egypt won the 1973 Ramadan War.

## IRAQ RETAKES BASRA

Once while visiting Jordan during the 1980–1988 Iran-Iraq War, I was watching an Arabic news program extolling the victories of the courageous Iraqi Army for having retaken the city of Basra from Iranian forces "for the third time." This story in the Arab press showed courage, valor, battlefield cunning, and skill and bestowed honor on the house of Iraq and the *Ummah al-Arabiyyah*. To my Middle Eastern way of thinking, I saw the merits of the story and how it played well for restoring honor and dignity in the Arab world. To my Western military mind, I thought if Iraqi forces retook Basra for the third time, they must have also lost it at least twice before! Then I realized that was immaterial to the principal issue, which focused on the restoration of honor and pride, and the elimination of dishonor and shame, upon the house of Iraq and the *Ummah al-Arabiyyah*.

## IRAQ WON THE 1991 GULF WAR

The 1991 Persian War, or Arabian Gulf War, was also known by the name Desert Storm. In August 1990 Iraq invaded, occupied, terrorized, raped, tortured, murdered, and took innocent Kuwaiti citizens prisoners who were never to be heard from again. The world community of nations, led by the United States, together with every Arab country (except Libya and Yemen and Palestinian-Arabs scattered throughout Israel and the Arab world) first demanded Iraq withdraw its forces from Kuwait. Then in a rare world coalition, these nations attacked and rained unquestioned defeat upon Iraq. However, before withdrawing his forces, Iraq's dictator, Saddam Hussein, ordered his retreating and defeated military forces, which had already raped, pillaged, looted, and plundered Kuwait, to unleash the largest deliberate manmade ecological disaster ever by setting fire to all of Kuwait's oil wells. After Iraq's defeat, Iraq willingly signed instruments of surrender, agreeing to cooperate with the international community through the United Nations, to account for and destroy all its weapons of mass destruction and their delivery systems, including biological, chemical, nuclear, and intercontinental ballistic surface-to-surface missiles (SCUDs).

A few years later when United States President George H. Bush, who presided over Iraq's defeat on the battlefield, lost the presidential election, Saddam Hussein celebrated. Why? Because all of the Western world leaders who had waged war on him, Saddam Hussein, were now no longer in power in their democratic governments. But he, Saddam Hussein, the tyrant of Iraq, was still in power. He felt vindicated. In his warped way of thinking, he held out the longest and was still at the top of his heap. Saddam Hussein could now hold his head high and have honor restored to his name. He, in his narrow mind, could now crawl out from under the rock of shame brought upon him by having lost on the battlefield of Desert Storm. There was certainly no feeling of guilt on the part of the Butcher of Baghdad for having invaded Kuwait, only shame for having lost the war, which was, in his mind, now lifted. He reasoned that after the world had unleashed everything it had in the way of state-of-the-art, technologically sophisticated electronic wizardry and weaponry, it still did not dislodge him from power, while all the Western world leaders who ganged up on him were now gone. Regardless of the fact that unseating him from power was never a war objective, he could now claim, though based on faulty reasoning, that he had won the Gulf War.

# Four

# Ultimate Fatalists

One only needs to spend two minutes in an Arab country before hearing the three words, often pronounced as one, *Inshallah*. The three Arab words are: *In sha' 'Allah*, Arabic for "If God desires," or "If God wills," or simply "God willing." Although it permeates all Arab speech today, those using it literally mean they will do something only if it is God's desire or will. This is true even though the one making the response uses the term mechanically and automatically. To Arabs, it has simply become a way of saying yes, and that is the way it should be interpreted when heard by Westerners.

*Inshallah* is used in response to any request, such as: "Can you give me a receipt," "May I have a doctor's appointment for tomorrow at eight o'clock," "May I withdraw $100 from my account." As Westerners, we are somewhat puzzled by such a response, especially if one is due a receipt, and one knows the appointment for eight is open, and it is one's own money one is asking to withdraw. But to the Arab, the ultimate fatalist, no event ever takes place unless it is the will of *Allah* (God); without God's blessing nothing happens. In practice, if one had an eight o'clock doctor's appointment and for whatever reason the appointment did not take place, then it must not have been God's will. If the reason for the cancellation of the appointment was because the doctor had been involved in an automobile accident on the way to the office, to the Arab it must not have been in God's great plan for the appointment to have taken place. The Arab perspective on fatalism is ultimate predestination. The following are examples of Arab fatalism.

## DRIVERS AT SEVEN O'CLOCK

I once traveled to the Middle East and Africa with the United States Air Force Chief of Staff as his Arabic translator, interpreter, and briefer. Following the first day's activities in Cairo, I was asked by the Chief of Staff's aide (a colonel) to advise the head of the transportation office for the Egyptian Ministry of Defense that we needed vehicles to be ready the next morning promptly at seven o'clock for the day's appointments. After translating the request, the colonel asked me what the response was. I responded that the officer in charge said they would be ready the next morning at seven o'clock, God willing (*Inshallah*). The American colonel insisted I repeat the demand to the Egyptian officer to have all cars and drivers assembled by six-thirty the following day for a seven o'clock departure. I did, and the response again was *Inshallah*. When the colonel heard the repeated response, he demanded I tell the Egyptian officer that it was God's will that he and all the other drivers and their cars be assembled by six-thirty the next day. Once again my words were met with the same response, *Inshallah*. I explained to the American colonel the cultural meaning of the response and assured him that short of an act of God, all drivers and cars would be there the next morning.

Suppose for one moment that one of the drivers did not show up the following morning for whatever reason—sickness, his death, the death of a family member, or a road accident. What would be the Egyptian-Arab cultural explanation for his not being there? Of course, it would be that it was not the will of God for that specific driver to be at the designated location for reasons mortals are not supposed to understand. As a matter of fact, the morning we left Egypt, we were told the Egyptian Air Force commander whom I had briefed the day before had died that night of a heart attack. The correct Arab cultural response was that it was God's plan for that man's life to end when it did. It is all part of God's plan: birth, death, and all of life's other events in between. To Arabs, events always occur as they do because God so ordains them.

## FAT OR THIN

Being an ultimate fatalist can easily explain much of the world around us and give blame or credit to God for things beyond our understanding, control, and even at times, our ambition. An example would be the difference between someone who has a slow metabolism and gains weight easily and someone who has a fast metabolism and eats anything but never gains weight. The fatalist Arab explanation is "It is God's will that I be fat," or "It is God's will that I be thin." This is a convenient excuse, a Westerner might say, for the overweight person who is not willing to sacrifice and take the required disciplinary steps to eat less or exercise sufficiently to lose weight. But to the Arab, everything is *min Allah* (from God). When one gets sick or when one dies, the very first response from Arabs when extending sympathies is *Heikbiddu Allah* (This is what God wants); in other words, it is the will of God.

## RICH OR POOR

This reasoning is also used by Arabs to explain their economic status. If they are poor, they first thank God for their blessings, then declare *kull she min Allah* (Everything is from God). This kind of thinking is also applied by some Arabs who look at the current wealth enjoyed by many oil-rich Arab countries. They reason that if God did not approve of them as a people, and if God had not wanted them to have personal wealth, He would not have given them oil. Today's wealth in the Arab world, a result of the great oil riches with which God has blessed the Arabs, is viewed by some as a sign of vindication or God's approval of the Arabs and their Islamic religion as being valid, the truth.

Many Westerners have great difficulty with this kind of reasoning since we in the West like to think we have some control over events in our lives, especially actions that we know will result in positive or negative effects. On the negative side of the cause-and-effect equation, we smoke, overeat, consume alcohol excessively, and on the positive side, we exercise, eat healthy meals, and take vitamins and minerals. Medicine and science have taught us that there is a direct correlation between certain activities and behavior which we can control. However, Arabs are not the only people to have a fatalistic perspective. Many Americans and other ethnic groups around the world share the view that God controls every event in every life, although modern medicine and science have caused some people to make minor adjustments in the fatalistic view of life. Modern medicine has also discovered that to a large extent it is one's genetic makeup that determines much of who we are, including our mental and physical potential and capacity. Medical science is also beginning to discover who among us are genetically predisposed to contract terminal diseases such as cancer and thus determine how long we might live. These discoveries add credibility to the Arab cultural prescription that who we are is divinely preordained.

A totally fatalistic perspective fosters a position of nonaccountability and blamelessness, which enjoys certain popularity not only in the Arab culture, but in the West as well. If God is to receive the ultimate credit for everything that exists and all that occurs in life, then how can people be held accountable for events which are preordained by The Creator and by forces far greater than any influence mere mortals could bring to bear? We even see this credit-blame and denial syndrome practiced by some of our most senior and powerful elected officials, especially politicians. Arabs by no means have a monopoly on deflecting blame.

Nevertheless, my observation is that Arabs as a group have more difficulty accepting responsibility than do other groups; it always seems to be someone or something else's fault. Road accidents often get blamed on events or conditions other than the driver, such as the weather, road conditions, the brakes, or other mechanical problems. Since shame is also a product of negative culpability, one can see how, in a society which places much emphasis on avoiding shame and dishonor, one would strive hard to deny blame for having done something negative. In the Arab world, parents are notorious for quickly coming to the defense of their children with excuses for reasons their child failed a test, or was forced to repeat a grade, or injured himself. Mothers and fathers make excuses for their children, believing their little angels could not be responsible for a single misdeed. Arabs, as adults, are also notorious for deflecting personal blame and making excuses for their own failures and shortcomings.

Among my favorite examples are the wild, unbelievable excuses people or their lawyers give for why they or their clients committed murder. Excuses and reasons I have read about for murder in the Arab world are "She wouldn't cook my favorite meal," or "She wouldn't clean the house," or "He wouldn't pay me money he owed me," or "It was an accident, I thought he was someone else." I suppose a judge's response to all these excuses or reasons should be "Oh, so that's why you killed. In that case it's okay; it's not your fault; we thought you did it out of deliberate calculation and malice."

Again, Arabs do not have a monopoly on these kinds of excuses. From an Arab perspective, the West, especially the United States, appears to be the world leader today for coming up with defenses for having committed social infractions and crimes. Arabs would argue that with the help of its legal system, the United States allows its people and their lawyers to concoct legally acceptable excuses for why someone may have committed a felony, including murder. With the help of modern psychiatry, criminals in the United States are able to successfully excuse away murder and even shift the blame to others, such as their parents for having overdisciplined or underdisciplined them as children or incorrectly administered other aspects of their upbringing, such as toilet training. When Arabs witness this aspect of the American legal system, they do not come away convinced that the West is a more advanced society. As we can see from the examples above, the phenomenon of deflecting blame is a universally shared human characteristic and not necessarily unique to Arabs.

## SUPERSTITIOUS AND CONSPIRATORIAL

In addition to being suspicious as a group, Arabs are superstitious and conspiratorial (Chapter 2, "Social Character"). Their superstitious and conspiratorial nature is a spin-off of their fatalism; that is to say, everything is done for a reason and is masterminded. Nothing occurs in a vacuum; everything is preordained and controlled. Because of their fatalistic nature, it is easy for Arabs to make the leap from divine intervention on the universal scale to human intervention on the international scale. As with fatalism, if nothing occurs without its being ordered and controlled by a higher power, then everyday events can also be explained and understood as being ordered and controlled by human powers.

Arabs especially explain world events as being controlled by great military powers for self-serving political reasons. They particularly like to credit (or blame) the United States, with its military and technical might, for events which are not fully understood or events whose apparent explanations are either politically or culturally unacceptable to Arabs. Arabs also like to blame the intelligence services of various countries for controlling world political-military events. A favorite target for their blame or credit, in addition to the

CIA, is Israel's intelligence arm, the Mossad. Conspiracy theories in the Arab world blaming the CIA and/or the Mossad for an international incident take on a life of their own long before all facts are known and long before all relevant facts have been thoroughly investigated. An example is the crash of Egypt Air flight 990 in November 1999. Within two days of the event, rumors in cities all across the Arab world were that either the CIA or the Mossad, or both, had deliberately shot down the aircraft because the returning Egyptian military men on board were carrying back to Egypt military secrets the United States and/or Israel did not want them to have. The most recent example of acceptance of the pan-Arab conspiracy theory and Arab deflection of blame is the September 11, 2001, terrorist attack on the World Trade Center and the Pentagon. The February 27, 2002, issue of *USA Today* reported that "an overwhelming majority" of Muslims did not believe Arabs were responsible for the September 11 terrorist attacks on the World Trade Center and the Pentagon. The majority of the respondents to the survey also disapproved of the American and coalition attacks on the Taliban and al-Qaida in Afghanistan. In spite of evidence that most of the hijackers were Arabs, only 18 percent of the respondents believed the attacks were perpetrated by Arabs, and in fact, blamed Israel or the United States for the terrorism.

Fatalism, superstition, conspiracy, and deflection of blame are strong forces in the Arab culture and very much a part of the psyche of the Arab mind and thought.

# Five

# Social Interaction

### EMOTIONAL EXPRESSION

Arabs as a group are more open and demonstrative with their feelings in public than are Westerners. Arab men and women are not inhibited about displaying their emotions publicly to friends or strangers. Remember from Chapter 3, "Shame Versus Guilt," the importance of form and outward appearance. It is an Arab cultural prescription to publicly display emotion and show enthusiastic and exaggerated feelings of warmth and happiness toward one another. This is not to say that Arabs are loud in public; they may be loud and emotional in their expression of warmth when greeting one another but not when it comes to personal conversation. Do not confuse uninhibited outward displays of affection and emotion with loudness. Arabs maintain a social decorum of relatively low-keyed personal conversation when they are in public, especially around strangers (Chapter 2, "Social Character"). Arabs perceive Westerners as loud and uninhibited in public as they yell greetings and carry on personal conversation with one another across distances, not caring who hears what they say. Arabs sometimes interpret such behavior as rude and disrespectful.

On the other hand, Arabs do raise their voices and get emotional when arguing a political point or discussing an issue of the day. To the Western ear and psyche, Arabs appear to be arguing when, in fact, they may be engaging in nothing more than haggling over the price of a kilo of fish. By spending just five minutes in an Arab open air vegetable, fruit, or spice market, one can hear many "arguments." In reality, these are not arguments, just friendly, animated discussions between people trying to agree on the final cost of an item. To Westerners, this behavior seems odd and even feels uncomfortable and threatening as voices rise and emotions appear to flare. A Westerner would consider it bizarre to argue with the clerk in a grocery store over the price of a pound of sliced turkey, yet this is an everyday occurrence in Arab marketplaces. However, today there are more and more Western style supermarkets throughout the Arab world and no price haggling goes on within these establishments.

## GREETINGS

Public expressions of emotion are proudly, forcefully, and enthusiastically displayed by Arabs when they greet each other. When Arabs meet one another in their homes, offices, or on the street, they initiate a ritual lasting from thirty seconds to one minute, exchanging exaggerated pleasantries, inquiring about each other's health, well-being and that of their respective families, and are gushingly polite to one another. This is preceded by same-sex kissing, hugging, and hand-holding. Fraternal and sororal same-sex handholding may go on throughout and after the greeting, last during a brief conversation, and not end until parting.

Arabs are known the world over for having an uplifting, warm, kind expression or compliment specifically tailored for every human activity and event. Examples of kind greetings for a specific event are *Naeeman* (there is no equivalent English translation, but it is derived from the word pleasant), spoken after one takes a bath or shower, or following a haircut; *Mabrook* (congratulations) upon receiving a gift or promotion, or on the birth of a child; *Allah Yerhamu* (may God be merciful) upon someone's death; *Hamdillah Ala Assalaamah* (praise God on your safety) upon returning from a trip, and all other conceivable human activities, events, and situations.

It is important to always remember that the Arab cultural custom of hugging, kissing, and handholding during a greeting are reserved for same-sex members only. Never will opposite sex friends or acquaintances kiss publicly as is done in the West. Do not ever make the mistake, however familiar you think you are with an Arab of the opposite sex, of kissing him or her in public. If you should make this mistake and publicly embrace an Arab member of the opposite sex, rumors will abound about both your and your Arab friend's characters, and you will have done your Arab friend a great disservice. Warm same-sex expressions of friendship in public are the only accepted form of greeting in the Arab culture. When Arab acquaintances of the opposite sex meet in public, they may not even acknowledge one another lest they be observed and their actions misinterpreted. At most, they may only acknowledge one another with a polite nod, a short smile, or a word spoken softly, and always at a distance in order to not attract attention.

## IGNORE THE OPPOSITE SEX IN PUBLIC

I once was in the company of my wife (an American) and another American woman in the Arab city of Nazareth, when we came upon an Arab male friend. He and I greeted warmly, and he half-heartedly glanced in the direction of the American ladies and politely smiled, then carried on a conversation with me as though the two women were not present. Upon our ritual departure dialogue of extending regards to each other's families, the American woman friend said to me audibly but ignorantly, "Aren't you going to tell him to say hi to his wife?" I ignored her comment and continued with my departure warm wishes for his family and parents. After he left, the American woman, thinking I was a chauvinist, tried scolding me for not extending greetings to his wife. No, of course, I was not going to tell him to say anything in the way of a greeting to his wife. In his society and culture, his wife is no business of mine. In his society, I explained, his wife is not an object for public comment, discussion, or mention. In Arab society, wives are off-limits to unrelated male members, just as husbands are off-limits to unrelated female members. Even within families, unless there is a compelling need for inquiry, such as an illness, opposite sex members of the same family are, for the most part, off-limits. Any show of familiarity or expression of interest in someone else's wife or husband is considered inappropriate, intrusive, and possibly indicative of unacceptable behavior between two unrelated members of the opposite sex.

## "GREETINGS TO YOUR MOTHER"

I once witnessed a noteworthy example of inappropriate expression of familiarity with someone of the opposite sex in Jerusalem. I was in a souvenir shop wanting to purchase an item when a boy of about twelve years came in. The boy interrupted the conversation between the shopkeeper and me. The shopkeeper told the boy to leave, but the boy persisted. After the third time the shopkeeper told the boy to "get lost" and he again refused, the shopkeeper looked at the boy and said to him, "Tell your mother I said hi." The message was abundantly clear to the boy. His shoulders drooped and his body language indicated his mother's and family's honor had just been questioned and maligned. The boy immediately turned around and walked out of the store. As I explained above, if the relationship between the boy's mother and the shopkeeper was aboveboard, his mother would be none of the shopkeeper's business. In this case, the shopkeeper used the social taboo of familiarity between unrelated members of the opposite sex to insult the boy and get rid of him.

One last word on opposite sex greetings: Even when close family members meet in a public place (such as an airport) after a long separation, they will not indulge in Western style hugging and kissing. A quick embrace on one or both cheeks, even among close family members of the opposite sex, is all Arab culture allows, even between fathers and daughters, and mothers and sons. The reason for the apparent "paranoia" over a public expression of warmth and friendship is discussed in Chapter 8, "Honor." While Arabs lack in opposite sex public display of affection, they more than make up for it in same sex public display of affection.

## THE MANLY KISS

Arab men engage in a kissing ritual depending on the familiarity, relationship, and social class of the greeters. Those of equal socio-economic class will kiss either once on each cheek, twice on the same cheek, or once on each cheek then back to the first cheek. Of course, kissing need not involve lip to cheek contact, and air-kissing in the proximity of one's cheek will suffice. If one is of a lower social class and is trying to show respect to the other, particularly in Arabian Gulf and Arabian Peninsular countries, he may attempt to kiss the one of honor on or above the nose to show subservience, or on the upper chest or arm, near the shoulder. If the one of honor or higher social class wants to express to the one of lower social class that he considers him as an equal and not of lower status, then a display of one-upmanship may take place where each tries to kiss higher on the other's nose in order to show greater respect. A variation of nose-kissing is nose-to-nose touching, where the greeters touch or bounce tips of each other's noses back and forth several times.

## RESPECT FOR THE ELDERLY

Arab society and culture maintain great respect and public expression of honor for their elderly, a tradition and practice which seem to have disappeared from Western society. Family patriarchs and matriarchs are respected for the wisdom they possess resulting from their experiences and long lives. Arabs acknowledge the position of the elders in their culture and society as the most valued and the most honored within the family. This is readily seen in public when a senior male family member or clan or extended tribal member appears in a gathering of assembled males. All rise immediately and form a line waiting for their turn to show respect by greeting and kissing the family elder or patriarch. It is a refreshing and humbling sight to see, if you are ever so lucky to witness the event. This form of respect is instilled in Arab families from the time children are very young. Arabs are appalled by the Western custom of banishing the elderly to a nursing home. In Arab society, there is no uglier form of disrespect that can be shown to those responsible for the family's very existence than to put them away in a nursing home and to pay strangers to take care of one's living ancestors. It is important to remember that in Arab society, most women do not work outside the home, and two-income families are the rare exception, so there is always someone at home who can care for an elderly family member.

I once attended the engagement celebration of a friend's son in a Palestinian-Arab town near the West Bank of the Jordan. At this event, the guests would walk onto a stage where the engaged couple were seated and greet them with handshakes and same-sex kissing. (Some guests would also place an envelope with money into the hand of the groom-to-be.) When my friend and his wife, the groom's parents, approached the stage, their son ran down to meet his parents, not allowing them to walk up onto the stage where he and his bride-to-be were seated. When he reached his father, he fell to his knees, took his father's hands and kissed them in a display of honor and respect for all to witness and acknowledge. The West can learn and benefit much from this form of honor and respect shown and given to family elders in the Arab world. I cannot help but wonder if there is not a correlation between the low crime rate in Muslim Arab countries and their society's respect for authority.

## PUBLICLY UNINHIBITED

To see Arabs openly and uninhibitedly show their emotions in public, one need only to attend either an Arab wedding or funeral, and given the opportunity, I would recommend both. At funerals, both Arab men and women cry, wail, beat their chests, yell, scream, pull at their hair and clothes, kiss the face of the deceased, shout promises of vengeance to the deceased (if appropriate), and throw their bodies over the casket. All this is done with no regard as to how they may appear to others, or who might be watching and what someone might think of them; to the contrary, Arabs go out of their way to publicly show as much emotion as possible for the deceased. By so doing, they are expressing to the community how much they will miss the departed and how much the deceased meant to them. It is a form of showing respect not only to the deceased, but also to the surviving relatives. This is in contrast to how Westerners, especially Western men, might behave publicly at a funeral. Westerners, especially American men, are taught from childhood that it is not manly to cry. It is no surprise that men in America have a hard time expressing their emotions at a funeral or any other occasion. American men have to resort to expressing their feelings for a deceased loved one privately where no one will see their humanness and sensitivity; whereas Arab men are not so encumbered. Western society is more lenient towards women, allowing them to outwardly express their emotions of sadness and sorrow by crying in public at funerals and even weddings.

Weddings are equally a place where Arab men and women are allowed to freely express their feelings and share their happiness with the bride and the groom and their families. Here, Western society is a little easier on the American male, for he is allowed to show his happiness more openly than he is allowed to show his sadness at a funeral.

## PERSONAL SPACE

Westerners are said to have a personal space of about eighteen inches, or an arm's length. Personal space is that imaginary bubble of space around every Western individual, especially Americans, which is considered private, sacrosanct, and not available for uninvited others to enter and share without the owner's permission. When someone enters an American's personal space, the American feels uncomfortable, irritated, offended, and even violated. Elevators, where personal space can become challenged, are particularly a place of anxiety for Americans who cherish their privacy and wish to maintain the sanctity and integrity of their personal space. Arab personal space is much shorter than that of Westerners. Westerners should not feel violated or offended when a close Arab friend enters his personal space to embrace, greet, or to simply engage in friendly conversation. To the contrary, consider it a compliment if an Arab enters and remains in your Western personal space while engaging you in conversation.

In Western elevator etiquette, everyone enters and goes directly to the rear or sides of an elevator, looks stone-facedly forward, avoiding eye contact with everyone, and mystically stares at the floor level indicator as though hypnotized. Arabs, on the other hand, will walk into an elevator, face the captive assembled crowd, and literally be "in your face," trading garlic- and onion-breath friendly conversation with you until it is time to get off. Although this behavior seems offensive and impolite to Westerners, it is a sign of friendship and acceptance by the Arab, and should be viewed as such.

One other place where Westerners feel their personal space or right not to be touched is violated is in crowds, while walking in an area with other people (such as a sidewalk or grocery store), or in a bus, subway, or anywhere else one might encounter others at close quarters. In the West, if one should accidentally brush up against another person, the proper thing to do is to offer an apology or excuse oneself. An Arab would no more think to apologize for brushing up against someone than would an American not apologize for doing the same. Arabs view brushing up against someone as simply a cost of being in public; people simply unavoidably brush up against one another at times, it is of no consequence to them. As far as Americans go out of their way not to accidentally bump into someone, Arabs do not go out of their way to avoid it. Arabs not only do not go out of their way to avoid the bodily contact, they may deliberately brush up against one another as the most expedient and shortest distance between two points. I had just returned from a three-year assignment in the Middle East when someone at Washington's Dulles Airport accidentally bumped into me and apologized. The strangeness of the apology, which I had not heard in years, struck me as being so odd that I laughed to myself and thought yes, I must be back in America.

## WAITING IN LINE

Some people might think that waiting one's turn in line in the Arab world might be a contradiction in terms. By and large, the concept of waiting one's turn does not exist. Waiting in line is strictly a Western concept which has very little relevance in the Arab world. You may find yourself patiently waiting your turn in line for the cashier in a store, or even in a Western style supermarket, but if it is in the Middle East, do not be surprised if two or three people walk right past you and everyone else in line, show their one or two items to the cashier, present their money, and be served long before you are. This behavior rubs the very fiber of any Westerner raw because it clashes with everything Westerners hold to be fair and equal. I am not suggesting that when Westerners encounter this behavior that they allow everybody in the store who so chooses to get ahead of them. What I am suggesting is that Westerners observe this behavior, get comfortable with it, and then apply it as part of their own shopping habits. If it helps, think of it as an invisible express checkout lane, because in reality that is exactly the way Arabs use it. Rarely will you see anyone cut to the front of the line with more than a few items. Another reason some Arabs will go to the head of the line is that they consider themselves to be of a higher socio-economic class than others. Remember, even today there is an unwritten caste system in Arab society.

It is not only waiting in line at the supermarket where Arabs will cut in line. It happens almost anywhere a line forms (at banks, post offices, or government offices) and carries over to other social interactions and everyday activities, such as driving (see Chapter 6, "Road Etiquette"). Arabs think nothing of inter-rupting an ongoing conversation anywhere, anytime, with either a drawn-out obligatory greeting, to convey information, or to make a request. While Westerners, especially Americans, consider this action rude, Arabs would consider it rude not to stop an ongoing meeting or conversation to greet someone who walks in, and even consider it totally acceptable to wait on a different customer while waiting on someone else first. This is nothing to get upset about, you should just accept it as part of the Arab culture. After all, they would afford you the same "courtesy" if it were you walking into their meeting or conversation.

## No Is So Final

Arabs have a very difficult time saying "no," particularly to their friends. "No" is such an unfriendly word, so negative, so final. "No" does not allow for any waffling, maneuvering, or any other fall-back position. Instead of saying "no" to a friend, Arabs will say "I'll see," *Inshallah*, (God willing), "I hope so," "If I can," or "I'll see what I can do." On the other hand, if they really want to say "no" politely and kindly, they will say something such as, "These things are difficult" or "It is not easy," or they will almost say no by saying, "My hands are tied," or "It's out of my hands," or "I would have if I could."

My most notable personal experience with Arabs refusing to say "no" occurred when I was designated and trained to be the United States Defense Attaché to Damascus, Syria. Out of consideration for Syrian sensitivities (hatred) toward Israel, and their not wanting to associate with anyone who had connections to Israel, it was decided that I should not conceal from them the fact that I had been raised in Israel and had served as the Assistant United States Air Attaché to Tel Aviv. This decision was made with the risk and the understanding that the Syrians would have difficulty accepting me for having served in an official capacity in Israel. Syrian (and therefore Arab) reasoning and logic would conclude that if they, the Syrians, allowed a United States official to work in Syria after he had served in Israel, it would be tantamount to Syria giving de facto recognition to Israel. The person who served in Israel under Israeli rule as a sovereign country had conceded authority and legitimacy to the State of Israel to govern in what Syria considers to be occupied Palestine. This perception may seem a little myopic from Western perspectives, but not from the Syrian perspective, and that is what matters. I am also sure that some Syrian official might have been concerned that since I grew up and served in Israel, there was the possibility that I may have been co-opted by the Israelis and was, in fact, an Israeli spy.

I, still in the United States awaiting word from Damascus that the Syrian government had agreed to accredit me diplomatically, was never told the specific wording used by the Syrians in their communication with our State Department officials at our embassy in Damascus. I repeatedly asked my desk officer for the Syrians' exact words to our embassy officials, and I was repeatedly told the Syrians were stating that everything would work out, but that it would take some time. I wish I could have been told the exact Syrian-Arab language used. As it turns out, our people in Damascus were being told "These things are difficult," "These things take time," "We are doing what we can," "*Inshallah*." Of course, as we all know now, the Syrians were telling us "no" all along, while not directly to our faces saying "no." Our diplomats in Damascus were also being given the run-around by the Syrians when asked for the status of my accreditation and were being told such things as the Defense Ministry had the request, or that the Foreign Ministry had the request, or that the request was at the Presidential Palace.

Six months after my bags were literally packed and sitting by the front door of my home, and while still awaiting word that my visa had been approved, and after I had bought two years' supply of all kinds of household provisions and personal supplies, and six months after my household goods had been picked up from my house by the shipper, the following event took place. The United States Ambassador to Syria asked the newly appointed Deputy Chief of Mission (DCM) to inquire into my accreditation when she made her first official call to the Syrian Foreign Minister. The newly appointed DCM said to the Syrian Foreign Minister, "We are still awaiting your positive response to the accreditation of our Defense Attaché, Colonel Baker." She received the following response from the Syrian Foreign Minister, "We have no intention of responding to your request regarding this matter, and you should read the appropriate diplomatic language into our response." After telling us an Arab "no" for six months but our not understanding the cultural language, the Syrians had to actually hit us between the eyes with a verbal two-by-four, and come right out and say "no." Culturally, they could not have responded with a direct "no" to us. After all, we were their friends of sorts, and we were attempting to broker a deal for them to get back the Golan Heights they had lost to Israel twenty-eight years earlier in the June 1967 Six-Day War. Their final "no" to us must have been very difficult, but perhaps saying no to the newly appointed DCM was easier because she was female.

We must listen very carefully to what our Arab friends are telling us. Sometimes they are saying "no," but we are not listening.

# Six

# Social Etiquette

e very society has its own set of social norms, mores, and customs which characterize it and distinguish it from other societies as a unique culture. Arabs and their culture have many customs and mores which are so very different from Western culture, that Westerners who want to travel, live, and especially those who want to do business in the Middle East must learn about, understand, and heed the specific social prescriptions that characterize Arab culture. This chapter is devoted to those everyday cultural and social nuances within Arab society that not only differ from Western culture, but which shape and distinguish Arab society. What follows are some seemingly harmless everyday activities, which if committed or omitted, would be insulting to an Arab, or at the very least seem crude and show a lack of consideration or respect toward the Arab. Understanding the following topics will help the Westerner become more acceptable to the Arab and facilitate better Middle East-West social interaction. Although some Arab habits and customs may seem strange to Westerners, it is important to remember that many Western cultural mores and customs are no less foreign and bizarre to Arabs.

## LEG CROSSING

Westerners, particularly men, like to comfortably cross their legs by placing one foot upon the opposite knee while sitting.

In so doing, one inevitably exposes the soles of his shoes to anyone who might be sitting opposite. To Arabs, it is a great insult to point the soles of one's shoes, or to expose the soles of one's feet, to another person. Westerners should always avoid this unnecessary, yet unintended, insult to their Arab friends and hosts. Although it is a difficult habit to break, it will have lasting negative repercussions if continued.

The following incident is a prime example of the way Arabs react to this thoughtless but insulting gesture. The former United States Secretary of State under the first Bush administration, James Baker, either was not told of this cultural taboo by his Middle East advisors (who should have known better), or they advised him about it and he was not focused enough to think it mattered to his Arab hosts and guests. I remember vividly on several occasions seeing photographs of James Baker sitting in front of Egyptian President Husni Mubarak with his leg crossed over the opposite knee and the sole of his shoe pointing in the direction of President Mubarak. Sometime later, I saw a photo of President Mubarak with his leg crossed pointing the sole of his shoe to the oblivious James Baker. Mubarak's action was a deliberate calculated reaction, not so much to return the insult to the clueless James Baker, but to send a message to the millions of Egyptians and Arabs, who were watching by television, that the American insult was noted and returned. Remember that honor, retribution, and the restoration of honor are paramount in the Arab world.

## Hand Use Delegation

It is imperative that the reader learn and remember this simple rule: In the Arab world, the right hand is the social hand, and the left hand is the toilet hand. This directive is Islamic-based and probably has its roots in early Arab desert cultural tradition. In pre-Islamic desert Arabia, water was a scarce and valuable resource which was not to be squandered. When available, water was reserved for drinking to sustain life. It would have probably rarely been used, or "wasted," for washing one's hands. Therefore, in the water-scarce desert environment, hand use delegation evolved as a desert survival issue, separating the two processes of personal hygiene from social interaction, using the left hand to clean one's self and the right hand for social purposes, to shake hands, share food, and eat.

The *Qur'an*, the Muslim holy book, specifies not only that one should use the left hand to clean one's private parts, but also how one should go about the cleaning. For this reason, Arabs never offer their left hand to anyone and never offer or receive food with their left hand. It does not matter if one is left-handed; in the Arab world the left hand is the personal hygiene hand, and the right hand is the social hand. One should never offer food to an Arab with the left hand. Arabs would first think such action to be crude, impolite, and rude, and would consider the food offered to be unclean since it came from the personal hygiene hand. If you are left-handed and you are eating with Arabs, sit on your left hand if necessary.

## PETS

Unlike the West, the Arab world has very specific social and cultural restrictions as to which animals are considered acceptable as in-home pets. These restrictions are partly dictated by the Muslim religion and are related to how Arabs view the hierarchy of life and God's creations. Hierarchically speaking, at the top of the universe and at the top of the pyramid of all life is God, all knowing, all powerful, all giving, and to be revered and feared (Chapter 9, "Islam"). Second in importance are the angels. A close third after the angels is mankind. The Arabic word for mankind is *Bani Adam*, or "sons (children) of Adam." After mankind, God created the animals and directed man to rule over them. To Arabs, most animals are dirty and disease carrying and are to be avoided, except in the case of sheepdogs for shepherding or animals raised for food or used as beasts of burden.

Cats, birds, and fish are the only acceptable forms of pets to Arabs. Cats have a special place in Muslim culture because of a legend regarding a cat which showed the Prophet Muhammad the location of a well in the desert which saved his life. Dogs, however, are considered unclean and are not to be allowed into one's home. Dogs are only acceptable as watchdogs or police dogs. If you are going to live in the Middle East for a period of time and you own "man's best friend" and insist on taking it with you, it would be best to keep the furry family member out of your house, or at least in a closed-off room while you entertain your Arab friends in your home. Arabs are quite amused at our attachment to our dogs and make all kinds of assessments and conclusions about Westerners and our sense of reality when they see how we spend billions of dollars every year grooming, feeding, dressing, healing, and even burying our dogs and our other pets in pet cemeteries. Such actions cause Arabs to some-times think that we have lost all sense of reality and even our sanity.

Although one might assume as much, the following are totally unacceptable as pets to Arabs, and Westerners should keep them out of sight if they have them: snakes, all rodents (rats, mice, and guinea pigs), and pigs. Of this group, pigs are the most offensive and least acceptable. Islam, like Judaism, prohibits eating pork or having anything to do with pigs. Pigs are considered vile, filthy, and repulsive. Needless to say, never serve or offer any pork product to a Muslim. If you have any of the above named pets, it would be best not to even bring them up in a conversation; your house pets will not endear you in the least to your Arab friends. If a Muslim or Arab wanted to insult another person, he would either call him a *kafir* (heathen), or equally insulting, *kalb* (dog), or most offensive, *khanzeer* (pig). It just does not get much worse. A word to the wise: keep your pets, and especially your pet pig, to yourself.

## HOME VISITATION

It is not realistic to expect to be invited to an Arab's home early in a friendship. Before Arabs are ready to come visit you in your home or have you visit them in theirs, they need to feel good about you as a person before taking the friendship to this next important level. I recommend that you do the inviting first, but not too early in the friendship. Wait until you have a good relationship with your Arab friend, either socially or professionally. When you do invite an Arab to your home, do not expect him to come with his wife, even if you have extended the invitation to her. He may even give you the impression that his wife might accompany him to your house by saying *Inshallah* (God willing), but she probably will not come. Do not draw too much attention to the fact that she did not accompany him, just politely remark that perhaps she can come next time. Also, if and when you are invited to an Arab's home, ask if the invitation is for you alone or if the "family" is invited also. "Family" is the usual euphemism for wife. Make certain you know the nature of the invitation, and whether it is for coffee and snacks or a full dinner. If it is an evening sit-down dinner, make sure you know what time to show up and keep in mind it will be a late evening and a short night for you.

If it is a dinner, expect to be offered a cold drink upon arrival, a custom which is probably a carry-over from the desert culture of offering a cool refreshment from the hot sun. There may also be plates of nuts and seeds as appetizers. The main meal may include perhaps two or three varieties of meats which may be chicken, lamb, goat, beef, or fish, and for special celebrations in the Saudi Peninsula, even camel, which tastes somewhat like beef. Camel served is usually less than a year old and is fed milk much of its life in order to keep the meat tender, much the same way we do veal in the West. The meal always includes mounds of delicious rice, and sometimes the meat is served on a large bed of rice on a huge platter, especially if camel is being served. In that case, the neck, legs, and tail are cut off, and what is served is the camel's torso, including the hump.

Other dinner dishes will include potatoes (scalloped or fried) and other vegetables, which may include rice and meat-stuffed squash, eggplant, grape and cabbage leaves; various salads (some unfamiliar to Westerners) made with garlic, onion, lemon, cracked wheat, barley, and eggplant; goat milk cheese, yogurt, pickles (including pickled radishes and beets), and black and green olives; and piles of warm, delicious Arab bread. Dessert may include a heavy sweet dish and pastry followed by fresh fruit. Coffee is the last item to be served. When offered coffee, you should drink at least one cup, which is usually served in a demitasse less than half full. Having a second cup of coffee is acceptable, but not obligatory. You know it is time, or at least acceptable, for you to excuse yourself and go home after the coffee is served. When you are served coffee in the Arabian Peninsula, and you do not want a refill, either so state, or simply shake the coffee cup back and forth three to four times when the server comes to refill your cup. He will then take your cup and not offer again.

✺

## GIFT GIVING AND RECEIVING

When visiting Arabs in their homes, it is customary to bring a gift. Never, ever bring an alcoholic beverage, even wine, as a gift to an Arab, especially a Muslim. Alcohol is strictly prohibited in their religion. That is not to say that there are no Muslims who drink alcohol. Even if you know the male member of the house to drink alcohol, do not embarrass and shame him in front of other guests whom he may not wish to know of his affinity for alcohol. It is perfectly acceptable, even desirable, and will ingratiate you to him, if you privately give him a personal gift of alcohol. If you choose to give him an alcoholic gift, make sure it is done in total privacy, and he will respond to your thoughtfulness and confidence with friendship and will most likely be more than happy to some day repay the favor.

When you visit an Arab in his home and you give your host a gift, do not expect the gift to be opened immediately, as is done in the West, nor should you ask your Arab host to open the gift. Receiving gifts is considered an embarrassment by Arabs, and they quickly put aside the gift as if to hide it and forget it ever happened. This they do because they feel embarrassed since they do not have a reciprocal gift to give. It is as though they are now indebted to you. From a Westerner's perspective, giving the gift is the least we can do to thank our host for his generosity and hospitality for having us as a guest, but from the Arab's perspective, his generosity is immaterial. What matters is that you have given him something and he is now indebted to you.

## ADMIRING POSSESSIONS

A fine line exists between being able to successfully give an Arab an admiring compliment about one of his possessions and not making him feel as though he should give it to you. Of course, if the possession is extremely expensive or large, such as a car or a house, there is little danger of his feeling obligated that he should give it to you. However, if the item is small and relatively inexpensive, such as a pen, lighter, or ornament, he might feel compelled to offer it to you and insist you take it. In such a case, you should graciously accept the gift and remember to return the favor with an appropriate gift at some point in the future. Rather than giving a specific compliment, a more general comment would be safer, such as admiring his taste in colors or arrangement or design. The safest compliments, and those most often given and cherished by Arabs, are those praising personal qualities such as kindness, generosity, intelligence, and compassion. Such compliments are freely given among friends and are considered good form and almost obligatory as the social glue which binds friendships and relationships.

## FAREWELL

At the end of an office or home visit, your Arab host will wish you a fond good-bye and will accompany you at least to the outside of his office area and possibly all the way to the outside building door. If you are visiting an Arab in his home, your host may make the comment that it is too early for you to be leaving, even though you may have been there for many hours and the hour is late. This is simply a polite gesture as though to say your visit was warm and your host very much enjoyed your company. Remember, form and appearance are paramount. After you insist that it is getting very late and you must leave (and you may have to insist), your host will not only bid you farewell to the door, but all the way to your car and will not go back inside the office or house until you have driven off. To wave good-bye at the door and go inside before you have driven off would be considered rude. Even in a place of business, the salesman or proprietor will escort you all the way to the door and wave good-bye as you drive off. This has happened to me many times, even while shopping for furniture.

Likewise, if you invite Arab friends to your home for dinner, snacks, a reception, or to your office, make sure you escort them to at least the front door or the driveway, and wave to them as they drive off. Of course, reason and common sense must prevail, and if it is raining, you need not walk them all the way to their car; escorting them as far as the front door would be acceptable. However, you must not shut the door or turn off the outside light until they have driven off.

## DRIVING ETIQUETTE

Sometimes the same rules which apply to the Arab manner of walking carry over to the way Arabs drive. It is common for Arab drivers to pull out into faster moving traffic if the opportunity avails itself. Their reasoning is that the road is wide, you who are behind can see their car which just pulled out in front, and you can move over. This flies in the face of American ideas of individual rights, of being on the road first, and therefore having the right to a specific lane. This can not only be dangerous from a Westerner's point of view, but will enrage many American drivers today to possibly take retaliatory action, ranging from a mild under-the-breath condemnation of the other's heritage, to a more visible hand gesture, or worse. To an Arab, it is a no-brainer. As Arabs see it, for the good of the group, you the individual have an obligation to change lanes so that others can also use the road. No thought ever enters into the Arab driving equation of having an intrinsic right to a specific lane just because he or she was there first.

The rule of thumb when driving in Arab countries is that the driver whose car is farthest out in front has the right of way. This rule is often called the "rule of the nose;" that is, if the nose of your car is farther out in front, you have the right of way. Another rule, which is the only way to negate this first rule, is if one makes eye contact with the driver who has the right of way. If you have the right of way, once you have made eye contact with someone wishing your roadway space, you have relinquished your right of way. The trick is to never make eye contact. The social forces which come to play in having to relinquish one's spot in traffic possibly have to do with Arab public politeness. If you make eye contact and visually "ask" to cut in, then an Arab has to do the polite thing and oblige you. For this reason, Arabs avoid making eye contact in congested traffic. But once they have, they smile and oblige.

Another aspect of Arab driving habits which is strange and sometimes frustrating to Westerners is how Arabs drive in two lanes at the same time. In America we call it "hogging the road." In the Arab world, it is simply keeping one's options open to shift to whichever lane affords the quickest access to getting further ahead in traffic. Related to this trait is the Arab propensity for waiting until the last minute to get in a single lane when the road narrows because of roadwork or lane blockage. Americans generally will begin forming a single lane of traffic as soon as they see a sign directing them to do so. Arabs, for the most part, will race one another down to the bottleneck, creating a bigger traffic jam, slowing traffic even more, and from a Western perspective, unnecessarily adding to a dangerous situation.

Arabs, like many other drivers in the world, have no patience when they get behind the wheel of a car. Unlike the rest of life in their society, when it comes to driving, they get in a big hurry, men more so than women. They honk, cut in line, and go around other cars, even if they have to go off the road, just to get one car length ahead of where they are.

Parking is another experience that will frustrate Westerners, in that Arabs may or may not adhere to painted parking lane dividers. In an open dirt parking lot, drivers will not generally attempt to follow a Western pattern of orderly parking where all vehicles point in the same direction. The local model will be random, me-first. Do not be surprised to come out of a store to find a car parked behind your car and blocking your exit. After laying on your horn, a surprised Arab will emerge, possibly smiling and wondering why you are so upset. Besides, he might argue (as has happened to me several times) he was only going to be a few minutes.

One observation a Westerner will make specifically in the Arabian Peninsula where oil wealth has allowed the local population not to be bothered with blue collar work or the service industry in general, is Arab drivers sitting in their cars outside a business, such as a dry cleaners or café, impatiently honking the horn for someone inside the establishment, usually a third-country national (TCN), such as a Philippino, Indian, Pakistani, or Sri Lankan, to come out and wait on them. This practice, for the benefit of Arab readers, is arrogant by Western standards. The TCN quickly runs out obligingly, waiting subserviently on the "country's masters." TCNs live and work in the Arabian Peninsular countries at the pleasure and mercy of the local Arab masters and are happy to be able to earn a few, sometimes very few, dollars to not only support themselves but primarily to send money home to their families. As a result, the TCNs behave as servants or slaves, always smiling to the landlords (the Arabs), always saying "yes sir," "yes ma'am," and asking if there are any other services they can perform. This subservient behavior, with its resemblance to slavery, affects Westerners, especially Americans, the wrong way.

A final remark about driving: Arab men and women wear some form of headdress, scarf, or veil which tends to totally destroy their peripheral vision. This impairment of peripheral vision, combined with the "rule of the nose" and slower cars merging into faster moving traffic, will ensure that Westerners will have a long and frustrating adjustment to Arab driving habits.

One last admonition: Before Westerners become too critical of Arab driving habits, they need to remember that it was not too long ago that most Arabs got off the camel, horse, or donkey's back and got behind the wheel of a Western contraption called an automobile. Arabs, for the most part, did not grow up with a long history of a gradual industrial revolution, with each Western invention adding to the national corporate knowledge base, culminating in logical and orderly vehicular rules of the road understood by all. The automobile, along with Western rules governing its use, is a relatively new introduction in much of the Middle East. The discovery of oil in the last two-thirds of the twentieth century has made car ownership a reality in only the last twenty to thirty years for the Arab masses, many of whom may not even be able to read and write any language, much less understand and adhere to Western or international norms and conventions governing the orderly operation of a motor vehicle. However, this generalization may not apply to Arabs under the age of fifty. Arabs, like any other people, bring to driving the habits and customs of their society in general, and therefore, some of their driving characteristics will reflect the greater society's mores, norms, and social behaviors.

Seven

# Doing Business in the Arab World

A society does business much the same way it conducts other normal social interactions; thus, the business process becomes an extension of the social process. All social prescriptions presented in the previous chapters (leg-crossing, hand use delegation, veneration of the elderly, personal space, the caste system, social identification, and especially the difficulty of saying no to one's friends) should be considered essential elements to conducting business successfully in the Arab world. All the restrictions and prescriptions that apply to everyday Arab society have a business application as well. What is good for the desert culture is good for the corporate culture. This entire book should be considered a business guide for the Western businessman or woman who wants to conduct business successfully in the Arab world. The advice provided in this chapter alone would be incomplete without a total knowledge of, and adherence to, all other guidelines presented throughout this book.

## THE INITIAL MEETING

When first meeting an Arab businessman, one must approach him and the encounter politely but reservedly. I specifically use the word "man" because men almost exclusively run the businesses of the Arab world. It would be extremely rare to encounter an Arab businesswoman. Do not assume that you or your product will be readily embraced and accepted by your potential client even if it is the industry-agreed superior product. Remember, Arabs are by nature suspicious of strangers and their motives. Be genuine, express all the pleasantries required, and be generous with your platitudes and compliments. Show you understand, appreciate, and most importantly, respect something of the Arab culture, history, and contribution to the world's corporate knowledge and discovery; it will reap you incalculable dividends and give you a competitive business edge.

During a first business encounter, following the required exchange of pleasantries, accept your host's hospitality of tea, coffee, cold drinks, or other refreshments offered. Do not refuse your host's hospitality by refusing his offer of refreshments. Even if you do not like what is being offered (such as the Saudi or Bedouin yellow coffee), drink it graciously. If offered a choice of coffee or tea, accept that which you prefer or dislike least. It is customary on the first visit in the Arabian Peninsular countries to be offered only the strong yellow Bedouin coffee, with no other choice. In the Levant, including Jordan and Egypt, the coffee is the familiar strong, thick, black Turkish variety. Coffee may be followed by tea. Of course, if you have a medical condition which precludes you from accepting and enjoying the food or beverage being offered, express it. Everyone understands doctor's orders, and if you want, you can use this restriction in your favor. Sometimes you are given a choice of beverages, especially an initial hot beverage, coffee or tea. If offered the bitter yellow Bedouin coffee, and it is more than your system can take, or if you have already had five cups of it that morning, then just say no thank you and ask for tea or water, whichever you prefer. Remember, do not refuse outright your host's hospitality. Similarly, if you are the host of an initial encounter, by all means offer coffee or tea and light snacks such as cookies, followed by a cool drink such as fruit juices and water. It is also perfectly acceptable for you to offer your Arab guests American coffee in your office since you would not be expected to have Arab coffee. You might also be able to ask for American coffee in an Arab office. There is nothing wrong with making your preferences known, as long as they are reasonable, and it may even give your host special pleasure knowing he is providing you with something you particularly enjoy.

❋

## HOSPITALITY AND RAMADAN

An explanation is needed regarding eating and drinking during the Islamic holy month of Ramadan (Chapter 9, "Islam"). You should always avoid eating, drinking, and smoking in the presence of a fasting Muslim during daylight hours during the month of Ramadan. If you are visiting a Muslim in his home or office during Ramadan, out of the Arab instinct and reputation for being gracious hosts, he will offer, or have a server offer you a beverage and perhaps some cookies or fruit or some kind of a light snack. This he will do even though he is fasting and will not partake of the food or drink himself. Even though he might insist that you help yourself, you should show respect for his religion and culture by graciously declining the offer. This is the only exception, unless as stated above medical reasons also mitigate otherwise, when it is acceptable for you to refuse an Arab's hospitality. However, if you do accept a Muslim's offer of food or drink during the month of Ramadan when he is fasting, and you consume it in his presence, in his eyes he has gained special favor with God because he has resisted temptation and sacrificed while you ate and drank. Therefore, ironically, you could be doing your Muslim friend a favor by impolitely and insensitively eating and drinking in front of him. My recommendation is to always decline the offer of food and drink in the presence of a fasting Muslim. It might not be a bad idea for you to also fast during Ramadan, especially if you are living and working in a Muslim country. If that is the case, you should then tell your Muslim host that you too are fasting and cannot accept his hospitality during Ramadan. By so doing, you have gained special favor in his eyes for respecting and accepting his ways. Why not fast during daylight hours in the company of Muslims if it will help you gain friendship and acceptance? After all, that is part of what you are trying to accomplish; additionally, it might be healthy to fast and cleanse your body from time to time.

## SUBJECTIVITY AND PERSONALITY DRIVEN

Arabs will do business with you not because they know or believe your product to be superior to that of the competition, but because they like you as a person. They will buy your product because they feel good about you and are comfortable with you. Friendships, trust, and business deals are not issues Arabs rush into. Friendships and feeling good about each other are a long and cultivated process. How unlike what motivates the West in business! The West is driven by such factors as higher performance, less maintenance, bigger, stronger, more efficient, healthier, better, less expensive. Although good performance and a superior product are important to the Arab, they are not his sole reason for buying one product over another, nor his single motivating factor. The human factor and character are what will decide the deal in the end. Western objectivity and logic are replaced with Arab subjectivity and personality.

## POLITICS

Together with the human factor are many other peripheral issues, such as the politics and the political leanings of the country attempting to do business in the Arab world. All this has to do with who you, the individual are, and whether the Arab even wants to get to know you well enough to do business with you. A good example of this would be the sale of a modern fighter aircraft to the Middle East. Much to the United States' displeasure, several Arab countries have in the past opted to buy what many consider to be the less capable French Mirage fighter, with its inferior avionics and radar and which lacks the war-tested stamp and overall capability of the United States F-15 or F-16 fighter aircraft. Why would the Arabs do such a seemingly illogical thing? Simply stated, politics. Some Arab countries like doing business with the French because the French are often less restrictive and less encumbered by politics. Arabs deplore the politics that come with United States Congressional restrictions on weapons sales because of the Israel factor (Chapter 10, "The Israel Factor"). Arabs consider it insulting when the United States refuses to sell them the same state-of-the-art fighter aircraft with all the sophisticated electronics and armaments which it is also selling to Israel. Arab countries assert that the United States holds the Arabs to a higher double standard as opposed to Israel. The bottom line is that Arabs ultimately will do business, or not do business, with someone based on character or personality or simply because they either like or dislike him as a person.

✸

## RUDE BEHAVIOR

The successful Western businessman in the Middle East will take the requisite time to get to know, befriend, and be accepted by the Arab. A first meeting should never be the time to present one's product line. The Western way of walking in for a nine o'clock appointment and by five after nine having notebooks open and brochures distributed will never work in the Arab world. In the West, we want to get to the point and not waste our host's time. In the Middle East such behavior is considered rude and will never reap dividends. Always let a first business encounter be a social call. On your way out the door you might indicate that you would like a second meeting to make some business presentations regarding your product line.

## HOURS AND WORK HABITS

Arab work hours, the workweek, and eating and sleeping habits and customs vary greatly from those in the West, particularly the United States. Arabs will go to work between six and eight o'clock in the morning, close down the office or place of business to go home for lunch around noon, eat a big meal, take an afternoon nap, and return to work around four in the afternoon and work until eight in the evening. Government and noncritical military personnel in some countries will not return after lunch; in others, the day ends around two-thirty. Arabs will eat perhaps the biggest meal of the day somewhere between nine and ten at night, and you as an invited guest will be expected to stay until around midnight. Americans who live and work in the Middle East have a hard time adjusting to this schedule since they are normally getting ready for bed at about the time Arabs are sitting down for an evening social event. The problem is that Americans work straight through from morning until late afternoon or early evening without the benefit of an afternoon nap. Weight conscious Americans also have problems with eating so late at night. Modern science and nutrition have taught us that in order to keep from gaining weight, one should not eat after six or seven in the evening, since these calories are not burned as quickly and efficiently during the sedentary evening and night hours.

In most of the Arab world, the workweek is from Saturday through Thursday, with Friday being the Islamic day of prayer and the only official day off. In some parts of the Arab world there is a move under way to make a two-day weekend similar to that in the West, with Thursdays and Fridays being the days off. As in the West, service industries, such as restaurants and grocery stores, continue to function on the weekends, but with reduced hours. Almost everything in the Arab world is closed on Friday mornings.

## PRAYER

The reader might find it odd to include a section on prayer in the chapter on business. This is not unusual if you have worked in the Arabian Peninsula, particularly Saudi Arabia. In Saudi Arabia (the most extreme of all Arab and Muslim countries regarding prayer time during the workday), government offices, including the military, stop what they are doing and go to the local mosque for prayer five times per day, even when the prayer time is during a scheduled meeting. For this reason, prayer times are usually published in the local English-language news-papers so that everyone is aware of prayer call and will not schedule an office call during this time. Of course, Arabs are practical, and special dispensation is given for skipping formal prayer call during war or national crises or when sensitive military or national security issues dictate. Even in the less restrictive countries of the Arabian Peninsula, depending on how devout the person is, meetings will stop or not be scheduled if they interfere with prayer call. Muslims take their religion very seriously, and the Westerner would be wise to understand this and be sensitive to the practices of Islam (Chapter 9, "Islam").

## ATTENTION TO DETAIL

Westerners are precise and exact. We need only to look at Western inventions such as the precision of a Swiss clock, the quality and dependability of a Mercedes, the rocket science of the United States space program, or the intricacies and attention to detail of the most complicated of all of man's creations, the United States space shuttle. All these inventions necessitate precision.

Western attention to detail can also be demonstrated in other ways. When giving directions Westerners, particularly Americans, will go into great detail; for example: go south 1.8 miles, down highway 95 out of Woodbridge, take exit number 53 to Dale City, go six stop lights and turn right at the Texaco gas station, go four-tenths of a mile and take a right onto

Western street. Arabs, on the other hand, give directions in generalities, not specifics: go straight down this road, you can't miss it. To Westerners, these simple directions are inadequate and incomplete. The Arab never intends on giving full or complete directions. His intent is for you to go down the road in the general direction of your destination, then ask for new directions and continue to do so until you reach your destination.

## TIME AND ACCURACY

In the West, when one has an appointment for eight o'clock, we are taught to not only be punctual, but to be early in order not to keep others waiting. We do it out of respect for the other party, and we call it punctuality and professionalism. In the Middle East, eight o'clock does not necessarily mean eight o'clock to the minute. In the Arab world eight o'clock means approximately eight o'clock, with a latitude of from fifteen to thirty minutes. A nine o'clock meeting I had with military officers from an Arab Gulf country did not get started until nine-thirty. Also, it was not until the last minute that I found out who would be in attendance from the Arab delegation; they had corralled a few men at only the last minute. The original Arab delegation, whom the United States had invited, never arrived. By contrast, the names of the United States attendees were passed on to the Arab host nation no less than one month in advance.

Attention to detail is a Western trait and not always a Middle Eastern concern or issue on which Arabs dwell. It is a reflection of the Arab cultural trait of being noncommittal and approximating. By remaining vague and noncommittal, Arabs can maintain flexibility and adjust as circumstances require. However, the Middle East is changing and is adjusting accordingly. Accuracy and attention to detail are requirements demanded by the nature of modern technology, such as aircraft, computers, medicine, and sophisticated modern weaponry, which Arabs and other countries produce, buy, and use.

The Arab traits of giving general directions, time approximation, and lack of attention to detail may have their roots in early Arab desert culture, when unmarked and uncharted deserts had no roads and only few landmarks. Directions in navigating the vast expanse of a desert devoid of distinguishable landmarks had to have been approximations at best.

✸

## FAILURE

Arabs have a difficult time with personal, national, or collective failure. Failure implies shame, shame implies dishonor, and dishonor is to be avoided, as we have seen in Chapter 3, "Shame Versus Guilt." At all costs, a Westerner should never directly tell an Arab that he, the Arab, has failed or has made a mistake or a wrong decision. Diplomacy is essential, and the approach should be oblique. A better way of telling an Arab that his decision or his answer was "wrong" would be to say the issue needs further work. One should make excuses, say it is a complicated matter and that you both need to spend more time on finding a workable solution. Explain how difficult the matter is; praise the Arab for his attention, effort, and talents in trying to solve the problem, but avoid telling him he made a wrong decision. Telling an Arab he is wrong or has failed is tantamount to saying "no" and should be avoided (Chapter 5, "Social Interaction"). If you tell him directly he is wrong, you will have insulted him and he will not want to have anything more to do with you, both from a business and a social perspective. Conversely, when the Arab has provided the correct solution to a situation, praise him profusely for it, exaggerate his talents, acumen, and capabilities. Your stock will rise precipitously in his eyes, and you will be favorably remembered.

Related to the notion of having difficulty accepting failure, Arabs sometimes collaborate during test taking at school. To the Westerner this would be fraud, cheating, and dishonesty, but not necessarily to the Arab. To the Arab it would be akin to not leaving anyone behind, giving true meaning to the term "cooperate and graduate." To fail is shameful and would reflect negatively on the entire group. Westerners particularly come into contact with this issue when Arabs are studying in the West. Even if an Arab fails a test or a course, he will most likely not tell his family back home who may be sacrificing to send him to the West to further his education. His family is already proud of him for being in the West and going to school. He has already brought honor to his family, so he could not disappoint them by admitting to failure. What often happens in such cases is that all concerned rationalize the whole Western education experience as being a difficult experience to the foreigner, the Arab, which it certainly is. They acknowledge that because of the need to master a different language, the whole experience will take longer, and difficulties, challenges, or "failures" may occur making the attainment of the degree take somewhat longer than normal. This is perfectly understandable. For an Arab to come to a Western country and earn a degree from an institution of higher learning is challenging and in fact should take longer. Language is a legitimate reason for significant difficulty along the way. How many Westerners, especially Americans, are there who attend Arab universities in pursuit of advanced degrees where the course of instruction is exclusively in Arabic? How long would it take an American to master classical Arabic to the point where he could earn a university degree? How many Americans, who do not have a language barrier as an excuse, are already challenged in their own country's university systems?

❋

## CHEAP GIFT

Gifts are given within the Arab business world as genuine tokens and expressions of friendship and fondness. Arabs, especially those in the oil-rich Arabian Peninsula region, give lavish and expensive gifts. By contrast, Americans usually give less expensive gifts often due to company or government restrictions regarding cost. Americans need to be more generous with their gift-giving and tokens of friendship. American gifts are sometimes embarrassingly cheap in comparison to Arab gifts. An Arab will possibly misinterpret a Westerner's intention based on the value of a gift, which itself may symbolize the value of the friendship. Having dealt with American companies and the United States government over the years regarding limitations on the value of official government gifts, Arab countries understand and sometimes make light of the value of gifts that we Americans can give and receive. Knowing the visiting American government official was not permitted to accept a gift over a certain dollar amount, one Arab government representative, upon presenting a gift to the United States official, once claimed: "This is a cheap gift from us to you so that you may keep it and not have to turn it in and be embarrassed, or embarrass us by having to return it." Fortunately, it was meant and said in good humor, but the message that the United States government was cheap was not lost on the audience.

As the business relationship grows, there comes a time when the Western businessman may need a decision from the Arab regarding the purchase of a product or service. Remember, if the Arab likes someone as a person, but is not giving a definite "yes" concerning his product or service, he might be saying "no." After a reasonable time of making a repeated offer, a hesitancy or a noncommitment by the Arab is definitely a "no."

## CONFRONTATION VERSUS COOPERATION

Westerners are driven by a sense of competition, individualism, self-reliance, and the American ethic of hard work and sacrifice to achieve a better life. Arabs are driven by a different sense of values that stress cooperation, consensus, group loyalty, and harmony. While the West believes in the direct approach for resolving disputes and conflicts, Arabs rely on the indirect approach, not only for arbitrating disputes, but also for facilitating business.

## WASTA

We Westerners are often in very unfamiliar territory when doing business in the Arab world because the West does not understand the basic and essential pillar of Arab social and business interaction, the intermediary. The Arab affinity for an intermediary, or go-between, for resolving and negotiating business deals is formalized through the institution of a *wasta* (the individual carrying out the *wasta* role is called a *waseet*), what we in the West call a middleman, agent, or broker. The role of the *waseet* is essential for any business transaction in the Middle East. Even more so than in the West, it is not so much what you know as it is who you know if a deal is to succeed. While I lived and worked in the Middle East as an official of the United States government, I always avoided disclosing to the average person on the street whom I had just met that I worked in the United States Embassy. The reason for this was to avoid having that person assume I could serve as his or her *waseet* to facilitate their obtaining a visa to visit or work in the United States.

In many Arab countries, there are laws which require any foreigner or foreign company wishing to do business in an Arab country to hire a local person or go through a local company as a partner and representative. Foreign companies may not do business within these Arab countries without local participation and involvement. This is what we might call *wasta* on a formalized grand scale. *Wasta* is required at all levels of society, whether it involves getting goods out of customs, applying for a passport, obtaining a driver's license, or other transactions; a facilitator is often a requirement. Certainly, it is possible to get the goods out of customs in the normal way, but one may have to wait three to four months for it to happen. When employing the services of a *waseet*, either a monetary remuneration is required or a debt is incurred, which can be repaid at some future time for a similar favor.

## COMMISSION

The West often frowns on paying an intermediary for simply making an introduction or allowing a deal to go through. In the Middle East, a business deal will not close unless an intermediary, a *waseet*, is involved. The West often has trouble with the fact that this intermediary, who might very well be of the ruling class or family, must be paid for simply allowing the deal to take place. If this kind of business practice were to be carried out in the West, it would be called or considered bribery or a kickback. In the Middle East, payments for allowing a business deal to go through are not bribes or kickbacks, but simply a cost of doing business. A better name for this payment in acceptable Western business and ethical terms would be a surcharge, service charge, a finder's fee, or a commission. Countries who understand such business practices to be acceptable (France, Russia, China, and others) do quite well in the Middle East. If American companies hope to compete successfully in the international arena, the United States government needs to understand this concept of intermediary payment and make sure American companies are allowed to compete on a level international playing field.

# Eight

# Honor

## MALE-FEMALE RELATIONSHIPS

As we have already seen in Chapter 3, "Shame Versus Guilt," the concept of maintaining or regaining lost honor is of utmost importance in the social psyche of Arabs, Muslims, and Middle Easterners. The honor of a man, woman, family, clan, tribe, and even a nation, is in and of itself cause to fight and uphold. We in the West say, "Without health one has nothing," while in the Middle East they say, "Without honor one has nothing." A person's self worth is measured by whether others perceive him and society as honorable.

In Arab society, the ultimate test of individual or family honor is placed upon the shoulders of the female members to bear and display. A young woman, and by association her family, is considered honorable if she has maintained her chastity until marriage. The older a young woman is before she gets married, the more suspect her chastity becomes. For this reason, some Arabs in the Levant (Lebanon, Syria, Jordan, Israel, and Palestine) have arbitrarily chosen the age of twenty-six as an unofficial cut-off date for acceptable single status for a young woman. After the age of twenty-six a young woman's chastity becomes suspect, and her chances of getting married diminish. Her value as an asset to a groom, and particularly his family and their honor, drop if she is older than twenty-six. A young Arab woman of twenty-two once confided to me that if she were not married by the age of twenty-six, she would have an affair. She probably reasoned that if society considered her chastity questionable and viewed her as "damaged goods" by age twenty-six, she might as well indulge since her chances of catching the eye of a respectable young man and his family would be diminished.

✸

## SEGREGATING THE SEXES

Chastity, the badge of ultimate honor in its unmarried young women, is so important in Arab culture that Islam and the Arab culture have established strict codes of male-female conduct and severe penalties for anyone who breaks these rules or taboos. First, in order to not present opportunities for violating the taboo, Islam and Arab society segregate the sexes from the time of puberty. It is considered inappropriate, and thus prohibited, for boys and girls to socialize or engage in joint activity, chaperoned or unchaperoned, after puberty. For this reason, Arab society often segregates education by sex after elementary school. In more conservative Arab societies, public education of boys and girls is segregated from the first grade. If a young girl belongs to a family that practices covering girls' and women's hair, this also occurs around puberty. Or, as an Arab woman friend explained to me, "We cover their bodies when girls begin to get their shape," approximately at the age of nine to twelve.

I once asked a Muslim Arab friend to tell me how to explain to my American friends why Muslims segregate men and women when they pray in a mosque. I explained Westerners, and practicing religious Americans in particular, view such segregation in a place of worship to be negative and indicative that somehow men and women are not equal in God's eyes. Put another way, perhaps women may somehow be viewed as not good enough to pray and worship alongside men. He first responded that all people are equal in God's eyes, and then added that men and women are not created equal; we each have different capabilities and talents and are given different roles in life which draw on our different capabilities. He then explained the reason men and women are separated (not segregated, he insisted) while praying is so that while they are worshiping their Creator and the God of the universe, no other distraction should be allowed to interfere with prayer. He then asked me, "When you were last in church and a beautiful woman walked by, or was sitting in front of you, and you could see her complete body shape, smell her sweet perfume, and see her beautiful hair and manicured fingernails, were you thinking about worshiping God?" Of course, I had to concede, my mind was not exclusively on worshiping God. He made his point.

## COVERING UP

Why do Muslim Arab girls and women cover their hair, and sometimes their entire bodies from head to toe (including gloves, veils, and/or masks)? First, my understanding from many of my Arab and Muslim friends is that the *Qur'an* prescribes that women should cover only their hair. Covering a woman's hair, face, and body is a cultural evolution out of a sense of modesty, not a religious prescription, and a practice that is believed to predate Islam. It is considered improper for a Muslim girl or woman to reveal the contours of her body to unrelated members of the opposite sex. It can also be inappropriate for girls and women to reveal their shape even to family members who are nonnuclear family members. This restriction is based on the Islamic-Arab premise that by nature a man is attracted to a woman's body, hair, skin, and smell. Since man was created to respond aggressively or sexually to a woman if her body, hair, or face were revealed to him, it is the woman's obligation to guard against exciting a man's natural libido. In other words, since man is created as a sexual animal in the presence of a woman, it is the woman's duty to ensure she does not do anything outside the confines of marriage that might arouse man's nature as God has created him. Westerners would think it is incumbent on the man to exercise self-control and treat a woman with dignity and respect, not to shift the burden of his weakness to the woman and then blame her if he fails to control his instincts and acts inappropriately toward her. With this kind of reasoning, it is possible for Arabs to use the defense that a woman was dressed provocatively and therefore "asked for it." This defense is hardly acceptable in the West but plausible in the Middle East.

In Islamic-Arab society, to ensure a man behaves himself in public and keeps his eyes and mind on his own business, women cover up their bodies in varying degrees, as deemed appropriate by individual or family interpretation and custom. As mentioned above, the most extreme cover-up is to completely cover the entire body in a loose outer garment (usually a black, hooded robe-like garment) called an *abayah*. To this is added a combination of a scarf and a veil covering the face, with the veil resting on the bridge of the nose with only the eyes exposed, or a headscarf with a mask that covers the forehead, bridge of the nose, cheeks, and mouth. This mask is somewhat reminiscent of a twelfth century English party mask, and is usually black or dark purple. Some of these masks are made of plastic and others are made of leather, with older women of the Arabian Peninsula usually wearing the masks.

❈

## ARAB VIEWS OF WESTERN WOMEN

Knowing how Arab women dress in public, what must be the Arab attitude or view of Western women? Western women in general wear clothing that accentuates and reveals the contours of their bodies. Western women wear sleeveless tops or shirts and low-cut blouses, often showing more than just cleavage. Western women, when relaxing at a picnic or while on vacation in the summer months, wear shorts, slacks, or jeans which reveal every contour and even more. Knowing what Arab society prescribes as acceptable dress in public, and the Arab perception of its effects on men, one wonders what Arabs, both men and women, must think about Western women's clothing and the message they are sending. They perceive Western women to be loose, morally bankrupt, and generally fair and free game for all men. This is most assuredly a hard indictment, but true so far as Arabs are concerned. Also, Arabs who have not had the opportunity to travel in the West get the information from which to formulate their negative perceptions of all Western women through the media, Hollywood, and television. Television series such as "Dallas" and "Falcon Crest" (in the 1970s and 1980s), "Baywatch," and "90210" (in the 1990s), and most recently "Sex and the City," as well as so-called reality television programs, such as "The Bachelor," have all contributed to the negative perceptions that Arabs hold regarding Western women. All these programs have made their way across the Atlantic Ocean and Mediterranean Sea, as have R-rated motion pictures and the James Bond movies.

Therefore, if one were an Arab from a sexually segregated (Westerners might say repressive) society, where one sees only the faces at most (much less the body contours) of only one's closest immediate female family members, what impressions might he or she infer of Western women? This perception is compounded by acceptable Western public conduct, such as passionate kissing, intimate touching, and the profane and obscene language used by both sexes. What conclusions might one come away with? Arab men often come away with the impression that all Western women want them for the asking. Unfortunately, there are enough Western women who are only too eager to oblige visiting Arab men often enough, and the myth, or rumor, continues to be accepted as fact, especially when money is provided in exchange for sexual favors.

What can Western women do to dispel this myth? The answer is simple: They should observe how Arab women dress and tailor their attire accordingly while living and traveling in the Arab-Islamic world. It is not necessary to cover up from head to toe, unless one is in Saudi Arabia, Iran, and until recently Afghanistan, but one also should not wear form-fitting, poured-into, tight clothing. A woman should wear sensible loose-fitting clothing which does not draw attention to any part of her body. The object of public dress for women in the Arab world is to portray modesty and to send the loud and clear message of nonavailability. At home, one may dress as one wishes.

✶

## MALE DRESS

Modesty in dress is not limited to only females in Arab society. Except for young boys and males engaged in sports, Arab men almost never wear shorts or even short-sleeve shirts, not even on the hottest summer days of over 130 degrees in the Arabian Peninsula. Except for their faces, Arab men in the Arabian Peninsula (including Iraq, Kuwait, Bahrain, Qatar, the United Arab Emirates, Oman, Saudi Arabia, and Yemen) are almost completely covered from head to toe, just as women are. The exceptions are military men, policemen, and anyone who wears a uniform while on duty. When Arab men go home, they revert to their traditional native dress, not too unlike Americans getting into comfortable jeans, cut-offs, and T-shirts when they go home.

In the Arabian Peninsula, the traditional Arab male dress consists of a white shoulders-to-ankles long-sleeved garment called a *thobe*. On his head, the peninsular male will wear a scarf folded into a triangle called a *ghutra* (or *hattah* in the Levant) usually secured by a double-cable black cord called an *'igaal*. Men usually wear a sandal or slipper-type of footwear. Depending upon the region, some men will wear a Western-type shoe. The male headdress can be solid white, a black and white checked pattern, or a black and red checked pattern. As a general rule, Palestinian and Syrian Arabs wear the black and white checked pattern, Jordanians wear the red and white checked pattern, and Arabian Peninsular Arabs wear either the solid white or the red and white checked pattern. Underneath the *thobe*, men wear white boxer shorts and sometimes loose, lightweight cotton long pants with an elastic waist, and some type of brief underwear.

In Egypt, with its mixture of peasant and urban population, men wear a combination of robes called an *abayah* in rural settings, and Western-type slacks, long-sleeved shirts and even ties and suits in the large cities. In Lebanon, Syria, Jordan, Palestine, and Israel, men wear a combination similar to that worn in Egypt, but less traditionally Arab and more Western. In North African Arab cultures, including Libya, Tunisia, Algeria, and Morocco, men wear a mix, with city dwellers in Western garb and rural dwellers in traditional dress, similar to Egypt.

## MALE MODESTY

No doubt the origins of the long sleeves and head coverings for both men and women have their roots in the need to protect oneself against the harsh Middle Eastern climate, where temperatures reach triple digits in the summer months, and for protection from the sand and wind which blast the unprotected body. Covering up in these harsh conditions is an essential issue of survival for both men and women. Later, the wearing of long loose clothing took on added cultural significance for purposes of modesty as well as for religious reasons.

Arab men avoid exposing themselves to other men in general, but specifically the area between the waist and the knees. The area of a man's body between his waist and his knees is considered a no-touch zone for other males, and is considered very private and off limits. No display of male patting on the behind, as is now the custom at Western sports events, is ever contemplated or would ever be acceptable in the Arab culture. Arab men are much more private about their genitals in front of other males than are Western men. As a result, toilet habits in the Arab world differ greatly from those in the West. One will not normally find a Western-style urinal in a men's restroom designed exclusively for use by Arab men. Neither will one find open communal shower facilities such as those found in Western gymnasiums, dormitories, or military barracks. Arab male toilet and shower facilities are exactly the same as Western female facilities: individual stalls with locking doors designed for total privacy.

## HAREEM, HAREM, WOMEN

The underlying intent behind the role and treatment of women in Arab society is to make them almost invisible to the public for their protection. In Arab society a woman's world is the private world of her family, and women are not to be publicly displayed, eyed, or mentally fantasized over by strange men. The woman's role in Arab society is in the realm of the private world, not the public arena. The West has often mistakenly used the term "harem" to describe a wealthy Arab ruler's many wives. This is a misinterpretation and misunderstanding of the Arab word *hareem*, invented and propagated by Hollywood.

In its most basic literal translation the English word "harem" comes from the Arab word *harram* (also *haraam*), which is the root from which the following words are derived: forbidden, refused, unlawful, taboo, honor, respected, venerated, sacred, and wife. The word "harem" in English is simply the plural of the Arabic word for wife, *hurmah*, its plural *hareem*, which also means "women of the household." Harem, or *hareem*, generally refers to the entire world of women and children within a household and can also designate the physical area of a house reserved for, and restricted to, women and children. In some Muslim and Arab societies the *hareem* was the area within a wealthy man or ruler's domicile where even he was not allowed to enter. In such cases his children, wife, wives, and/or mistresses would be brought to him in his quarters, or they would meet in a neutral portion of the castle, mansion, or estate. In Arab-Islamic society a man or ruler needed a safe place in his house, which was reserved for the raising and caring of his children and for their mothers, which was separate from the public portion of the house where outsiders and strangers could be received and hosted. This would be a place which was taboo, denied, forbidden, and protected from the uncaring, cold, scheming, and self-serving outside world. This place in a man's house was called the *hareem*, a far cry from the misleading Hollywood interpretation.

❁

## MARRIAGE AND DIVORCE

Although Islam's Prophet Muhammad had nine wives, he limited the number of wives his followers could have to four. Arab women, like their Western sisters, are limited to one husband (at a time). Some wealthy and powerful Arab leaders throughout history have gotten around (and still may get around) this limitation by divorcing one of their four wives and marrying another, maintaining the balance of four. There is no limit to how many times a man or woman can divorce and remarry. When the subject comes up, Arabs say that Western men and women are allowed to marry as many spouses as they want, with the only stipulation being that these marriages be sequential, not simultaneous. In the not too distant past, about twenty-five to thirty years ago, divorce was almost unheard of in the Arab world. Today, however, divorce is becoming more common. Headlines in a daily Arab newspaper recently noted the divorce rate had risen to over twenty-seven percent, a figure extremely high by Arab standards.

If a man chooses to marry more than one woman at a time, Islam is very specific about how he must treat his wives. In Islam, a man is to treat each of his wives with equality. That is, if a man has more than one wife, and he buys one of his wives a house, he must also provide the other(s) with a similar house, or arrange for them all to have the same amount of square footage within his house. If he buys a dress for one, he must also buy his other wives dresses. If he buys a television, shoes, food, gifts, or takes one wife and her children on a vacation, he must also treat all others equally. As a result, multiple wives are expensive, and therefore out of the financial reach of most Muslim men. However, with so much wealth in the Arab world these days, specifically in the oil-rich Arabian Peninsula and Arabian Gulf countries, multiple marriages are becoming more common. While stationed in the Arabian Peninsula, I personally knew several men with two and three wives. It was an interesting experience to go shopping during officially escorted trips to the United States with some of these Arab men. On one such trip with an Arab who had two wives, eleven children and counting, his shopping carts became full in a hurry. This same man always asked me before I returned to the United States to bring back for him the male sexual performance-enhancing pill Viagra!

As in marriage, Islam requires a man who divorces his former wife or wives to care for them and any children he might have had with them. Although the West (with the help of Hollywood) has shown it to be fairly simple for a Muslim man to get a divorce by simply saying "I divorce you" three times in the presence of a witness, in reality the financial obligations of divorce, as in marriage to more than one woman, are steep. Consequently, the average Muslim Arab man has only one wife, and most marriages last. It comes down to simple economics.

❋

## PLEASURE AND CONVENIENCE MARRIAGES

There are two relatively new types of "marriages" which have emerged in the Muslim Arab world. They are called *mut'ah* and *misyaar*. The first, *mut'ah*, simply means pleasure. To call *mut'ah* a "marriage" is probably too strong a term. It is more of a temporary legal arrangement than it is a traditional legal marriage. The purpose of this type of "marriage" is to provide a legal framework for a man and a woman to engage in a purely physical relationship with no strings attached. Both partners enter into this relationship knowing neither is legally entitled to anything except the temporary physical relationship and any favors or gifts they wish to exchange. In a *mut'ah* "marriage" neither the woman nor any children who may be born as a result of this "marriage" are legally entitled to the man's property, nor are the children entitled to his name or an inheritance. It is purely a legal arrangement for physical gratification.

The second designer marriage, *misyaar*, is also a temporary legal arrangement allowing a man and woman to live as married, even if the man has another wife or wives and other households. In this arrangement a woman may enter the arrangement with a specific purpose and certain needs other than just physical gratification. She may be a widow with small children who need care and feeding, but she may not have the financial means to care for them herself. Therefore, she enters into a legal arrangement giving the man certain marital privileges, while legally obligating him to care for her and her children.

Both the *mut'ah* and *misyaar* marriages are the invention of, and are primarily found in, the wealthier oil-rich countries of the Arabian Gulf. While both arrangements are designed to serve certain needs, not everyone is happy with them, particularly some Arab women. I have heard Muslim Arab women complain that both of these new "designer marriages" seem to take advantage of Muslim religious loopholes to serve specific pleasures of some overpaid, oversexed, and self-centered men.

❁

## CIRCUMCISION

All Muslim males are circumcised at birth. This ritual is performed for religious reasons similar to those of the Jewish faith. Muslims believe male circumcision was commanded by God to Abraham and all his male descendants.

I hesitate to even discuss the following subject of female circumcision because it is not a pervasive practice in the Arab and/or Muslim world; however, there seem to be a lot of myths associated with it as being a common practice within these cultures. First and foremost, female circumcision is not a practice either prescribed by Islam or the Arab culture. However, much attention has been given recently to female circumcision in some Muslim countries, necessitating some explanation to separate myth from reality. It is impossible to overemphasize the fact that female circumcision is not a religious prescription of Islam, nor is it an Arab cultural practice. Where it is practiced, it is performed strictly for regional non-Arab cultural reasons.

Female circumcision is more accurately female genital mutilation, and ranges from simple (if this barbaric procedure can be described as simple) clitoral removal to total genital amputation including clitoris and labia. This is then followed by total, or nearly total, vaginal closure with adjoining skin. Sometimes a small opening is left for urination and menstrual discharge. The procedure is often carried out by a village practitioner with little or no education, and most certainly no modern medical training, using nonsterile primitive cutting instruments. Consequently, young women who undergo the procedure, usually at pre-puberty, pass out from the pain since no anesthesia is used and may become seriously ill with infection and often die. Girls who do survive the genital mutilation often have complications later if they are sewn shut. Urine and blood back up in their bellies, resulting in infection, and they develop toxemia with high fever. Sometimes the young girls die if they cannot get qualified medical care in time. Those young women who survive all the hazards and marry are later traumatized as their husbands attempt intercourse because only a small opening exists with nothing resembling a normal vaginal opening. Some documented horror stories speak of husbands attempting intercourse several times before penetration is accomplished. The husband then brags as though it were an issue of honor as to how tightly shut his bride was sewn and how hard he had to struggle to "conquer" her, as though it were a heroic act of bravery on his part. The worst and most grotesque accounts are of husbands taking a knife to their young brides to open their long healed, shut, and lifeless vaginal openings. Of course, this often results in much blood loss, infection, and sometimes death.

Countries where female genital mutilation is most prevalent are Sudan, parts of Egypt (especially the southern part near the Sudanese border), and other contiguous African countries. Again, it is important to stress that although some of the people who practice female genital mutilation are Muslims, the practice is not condoned by Islam, nor is it a religious or Arabic cultural prescription. The only connection to the Muslim world is that some of its practitioners are Muslim. The practice is essentially nothing more than a cultural chastity belt for young unmarried women. Another reason for its practice is so that women will lose their sexual desire and will not be able enjoy themselves sexually, and thus would be less likely to seek pre- or extramarital sexual relationships. Some countries, such as Egypt, where this mutilation was a practice in the past, have gone on record to officially condemn and outlaw the practice. Unfortunately, such a law is difficult to enforce, and old customs and cultural traits are not easily changed by legislation. As a result, the practice continues in villages and cities alike.

❀

## HOMOSEXUALITY

As a result of the strict Islamic segregation of the sexes, there are often rumors in the West about the proliferation of homosexuality in the Arab-Islamic world. To set the record straight, there is homosexuality in the Arab-Islamic world, both male and female, but not always strictly as we know it in the West. No one has specific figures or percentages, but it is generally thought that homosexuality in the Arab-Islamic world is high. In a society that punishes heterosexual premarital sexual relations by death, there flourishes a measure of premarital homosexuality. However, there is a difference between Western and Middle Eastern homosexuality. Much of the homosexuality in the Arab world is nothing more than unmarried young adult experimentation and/or a safe sexual release not permitted by society in any other way. What also makes it somewhat different from Western homosexuality is that in Arab male homosexuality, the member assuming the female role is the only participant considered to be a homosexual. This is a novel perspective for Westerners but very logical for Middle Easterners. To the male assuming the male role in the relationship, the act is simply a release; it is the only two-person sexual encounter which will usually not get him killed. Usually, those males who engage in this type of homosexual activity will eventually marry, thereby confirming that the activity was nothing more than a temporary outlet.

Of course, as in all societies, there are life-long homosexuals in the Arab world. However, unlike what has become an acceptable alternate lifestyle in the West, homosexuality in Arab society is considered an issue of shame and is still very much in the closet. As recently as January 2002 there was a statement issued by the Saudi Arabian Ministry of the Interior regarding the beheading of three men who were accused and found guilty of "acts of sodomy, marrying each other, seducing young men, and attacking those who rebuked them." Arabs view with horror and repulsion Western acceptance and display of open homosexuality, which they consider to be unacceptable deviant behavior. The correct (classical) Arabic definition for homosexuality is "deviant sexuality." I once asked an Arab friend how I could best explain to Americans the Arab phenomenon of "temporary homosexuality." He answered, "After you've experienced the real thing (sex with a woman), you certainly don't go back to a poor substitute."

Undoubtedly, there is also active female homosexuality in the Arab world. However, since the subject and the act are so taboo and secretive and because I am a male and have no easy access to the Arab world of women, I have no reliable information on the subject.

## HONOR BY DEATH

As mentioned above, there are extreme penalties for breaking society's taboo against merging the sexes outside of marriage. In Muslim Arab society, if a young boy and a young girl were to secretly meet and have a physical out-of-marriage, intimate relationship, the penalty for both would be death. The young girl, if discovered, would be killed by her brothers and/or father, and society would condone the killing. By having an illicit out-of-marriage sexual relationship with a boy, the young girl brings dishonor on her mother and father's house and on her entire family. The only way to restore the honor is by killing the perceived perpetrator of the dishonor. After killing the young woman who brought shame and dishonor to her family, the young men, the father, and even the uncles and male cousins of the dishonored family, go after and kill the young man who shared in dishonoring their family. Although modern Arab police departments frown on such revenge killing and occasionally make arrests and hand down prison sentences for such actions, the practice goes on largely condoned because these police departments and courts are made up of men with similar mores and religious and cultural beliefs as the society they serve.

For this reason, girls and women in Muslim Arab society go to extreme measures to cover up their bodies to maintain their family's dignity and honor, and to send the message that they are not available for the unwelcome advances from strange men. I once was traveling by taxi from Damascus, Syria, to Amman, Jordan. I was sharing the vehicle with five other men, all of us strangers to one another. The last passenger to enter was a young woman, approximately eighteen years old, who was accompanied to the taxi by her mother. After looking into the taxi and seeing we were all men aged from our thirties to our fifties, the mother looked us all in the eye and placed the responsibility of her daughter's safety on each one of us. The mother said, "This is your sister, your daughter; take good care of her and ensure nothing happens to her." We were now all deputized as honorary family members of the young woman, charged with her safe passage. She was now pseudo-kin, and we had to defend and uphold the family honor. Not one of the men dared behave in any way other than with total honor and respect, and every one of us felt responsible to ensure that no one made any unacceptable advances toward the young woman. No one in the taxi said a word to the young lady the whole trip. She spoke only once, to tell the driver where to let her off once we reached Amman.

⊕

## HONOR'S BLOOD

Some members in Arab society, especially the poorer and less educated, go to extreme measures to find out if a young woman has maintained her family's honor until her wedding day. The practice varies from country to country, but the basic idea is for a young bride to present blood evidence of her chastity on her wedding night. Some practices require that the young bride discretely bring or send to her father and mother's house, and to the house of her new in-laws, a blood-soaked handkerchief, produced as a result of the sexual consummation of her marriage. Others, such as in North Africa, specifically Morocco, have the wedding party singing, dancing, ululating (a shrill performed by rapidly moving the tongue back and forth in the mouth), and clapping joyously outside the newly married couple's bedroom as they consummate the marriage. Upon completion, the bride passes the blood-soaked sheets to the wedding party, who displays them on a large brass tray paraded over their heads through town. The wedding party presents the "honor" evidence to the bride's and groom's families and to all of society.

Honor is very much alive and well, and a powerful force in Arab society. It is fiercely maintained, fought for, and proudly displayed.

# Nine

# The Essence of Islam

No thorough understanding of Arab society and culture can be complete without a basic knowledge of Islam and its founder Muhammad. Islam's influence and strength in shaping and controlling Arab culture has no equal. Islam is the reason Arab culture and language permeate a large portion of the earth we call the Arab and Muslim world or, as it is often called in the West, the Moslem world. It is estimated that there are approximately 1.25 billion Muslims in the world today, or one-fifth of the world's population, and nearly one billion people who call themselves Arabs. A fact that is not always apparent is that not all Arabs are Muslims, and not all Muslims are Arabs. For example, the largest Muslim country in the world is Indonesia, but Indonesia is not an Arab country. Also, the most populous Arab country in the world is Egypt with approximately five million Coptic Christians.

This chapter is not meant to be an in-depth exposition of Islam. There are numerous books on Islam by both Western and Arab scholars that provide far greater detail than is needed for the scope of our inquiry. Of note to the reader is that Western and Arab scholars do not always agree on all aspects of historical Islam. Generally, Western scholars attempt to be more critical and objective when discussing Islam as a religion, while Arab and Muslim scholars tend to treat the subject with more reverence, accepting their religion as the inerrant word of God. Arab and Muslim scholars avoid analyzing, questioning, or criticizing any aspect of Islam, historically or substantively. The scope of this chapter is intended to be a survey of the basic tenets of Islam and how it shapes everyday Arab society and culture. This chapter is designed to present to the Westerner what he needs to know about Islam so far as it might affect his interaction with Muslims and Arabs. I generally address the subject of Islam in this chapter as a Westerner looking at it from the outside with the intent of understanding and explaining the hows and whys of the religion, not from a Muslim perspective of unquestioned faith and devotion. Muslims believe all the teachings of Islam are direct revelations from God to the Prophet Muhammad.

## PRE-ISLAMIC ARABIA

At the time of the Prophet Muhammad's birth in 570 A.D., the inhabitants of the Arabian Peninsula and its principal city of Makkah (also spelled Mecca) were a Semitic, Arabic speaking, polytheistic people. The three most important of their pagan gods were *Manat, Uzza,* and *Allat,* who were ruled by a higher deity, called *Allah.* Each migratory Bedouin tribe had its own god represented by a stone, which the tribe kept in a tent and carried into battle much like the Jews revered and carried the Ark of the Covenant. The most important settled and established town in Arabia at the time of Muhammad's birth was Makkah. In Makkah each clan had its own deity stone, but collectively all the clans displayed their social unity with a common symbol of the large cube-shaped stone building called the *Ka'bah.* As with many other customs and habits of a desert culture, the religion of both the tribal and the settled communities was communal, not personal. Muslims today believe the *Ka'bah* to have been built by Abraham, and thus it takes on added significance and reverence.

Bedouin tribalism was the dominant social feature of the Arabian population where the focal social unit was the group, not the individual. As has been pointed out in Chapter 1, "Arab Identity," emphasis on the group versus the individual was an outgrowth of the need to survive in the harsh climate and environment of the desert. Politically, each tribe appointed a *sheikh*, or an elder, whose duty was more to follow the tribe's wishes than to lead. This so-called *sheikhy* leadership system developed into a monarchical system of father-to-son succession. Southern Arabia's main economic activity was trade: raising sheep, goats and camels, limited farming, and raiding rival tribes for revenge and booty. This was the setting into which Muhammad, the Prophet of Islam, was born.

## MUHAMMAD'S LIFE AND REVELATIONS

Muhammad was born into the Quraish tribe in the western Arabian city of Makkah in 570 A.D. He was orphaned at a young age and raised first by his paternal grandfather until his death, and then by his uncle. Muhammad acquired wealth and status when he married a twice-widowed distant relative named Khadijah, who was believed to be fifteen years older than he was. The usual figures identify Muhammad as being twenty-five and Khadijah as being forty years old when they got married. Khadijah and Muhammad had four daughters and several sons, with all sons dying in infancy, creating a serious succession problem following Muhammad's death because he had no living male heirs. While Khadijah was alive, the Prophet had no other wives. However, after her death, it is reported the Prophet had from seven to nine wives; sometimes he married for love, sometimes out of compassion for a widow and her children, and other times for political reasons. Muhammad's marriages to widows are defended by Muslims as humanitarian gestures to care for destitute women and to prevent their children from having to grow up as orphans. It is interesting to note that although the Prophet allowed himself as many as nine wives, he limited his followers to no more four wives at any one time. That is not to say that a man in Islam can only have married four wives in his lifetime. He can only be married to four women at any one time. Women on the other hand, can have only one husband at a time.

During his lifetime Muhammad engaged in travel and commerce, first by working in his extended family's trade business and later through his wife's trading company. These trade routes took Muhammad out of the Arabian Peninsula to what is today Syria and all points between. It was during these travels that the Prophet of Islam became exposed to the concept of monotheism and to the religions of Christianity and Judaism. Following his marriage, and as the beneficiary of Khadijah's wealth, Muhammad spent less time trading and more time in solitary contemplation of the world around him in the hills surrounding Makkah. He began having dreams and visions, which he later described as revelations from the one true God, spoken to him through the Angel Gabriel. At first he kept these revelations to himself but slowly began sharing them with his wife, who encouraged him to share them with others. Islam teaches that Muhammad, who like most Makkans of his day, was illiterate and was directed by the Angel Gabriel to "*iqra*" (read or recite; the word has both meanings in Arabic). Additionally, since the Angel Gabriel did not present Muhammad with a written text, it is obvious that in this context Gabriel's command could only have meant recite. What Muhammad was to recite were new revelations to the people of Makkah, the word of God, the directives of *Allah* (God), the Creator of all the universe and mankind. These revelations were prescriptions for righteous and godly living and for the acceptance and submission to the one and only true God, *Allah.*

The word *Islam* in Arabic means submission—that is, submission to the will of God. All who follow Islam are there-fore Muslims, or ones who submit to God's will. The Muslim act of prostrating oneself when praying, first bending at the waist, then falling to the knees, and finally prostrating with the forehead and face to the ground is symbolic of the total submission of the body and mind to God by the believers. After Muhammad's death, his followers assembled all his revelations into what is today the Muslim holy book called the *Qur'an* (sometimes spelled Koran). This *Qur'an* is believed to be, and stated by Muslims to be, the infallible word of God. The *Qur'an* is not to be questioned, translated, or interpreted, as that would be blasphemy.

The language of the day in Arabian Makkah was Arabic, as was the language spoken by the Angel Gabriel to Muhammad during the dictation of the revelations. This point is given as evidence of the legitimacy and validity of Arabic as being more than just a language equal to all others. The Arabic spoken by the Angel Gabriel is considered a sacred language, since it was believed to be the language spoken by angels in heaven. Arabic, Muslims deduce, must therefore be the heavenly language. For this reason Arabs revere, venerate, and lift up their language to be more worthy than all other languages. This is a fact one should keep in mind when one hears Arabs say it is impossible to translate the true meaning of the *Qur'an* into other languages since it would lose its true meaning as intended by God.

Early in his ministry, Muhammad had very few converts to his revelations and new way of life. Encouraged by his wife Khadijah to publicly preach his revelations, Muhammad began gaining followers very slowly. The Prophet's recitations and teachings called for all to rid themselves of their sinful ways and their pantheon of gods, and acknowledge and worship only one God as the only true God, whom he called *Allah*. Makkah's pagan polytheistic religious practices and its political system were being threatened by Muhammad's teachings of a whole new way of living. Muhammad called for social reform, caring for those who could not care for themselves, giving personal wealth to charity and welfare, and forbidding one to charge interest on loans. The new preacher had other prescriptions and limitations which irritated Makkans, such as forbidding his followers to drink alcohol and eat pork.

However, the Makkans' chief opposition to Muhammad was a combination of economic, religious, and political reasons. For one thing, the Makkans profited greatly from the hundreds of pilgrims who came annually to worship the plethora of gods housed in the *Ka'bah*. Were the Makkans to convert to the prophet's one-god religion, the lucrative religious pilgrimage to Makkah would dry up. Secondly, the desert Arabs of the Quraish tribe were delighted with their plurality of divinities, a veritable supermarket of gods. Finally, tribal politics was at issue. To lose control of the religious establishment and its accompanying economic power would be an open invitation for hostile tribes to attempt an armed challenge for power. For Makkan and Arabian society, Muhammad was simply bad news.

✦

## FLIGHT AND POLITICS

In the year 622 A.D. Muhammad and his followers, mainly young men of minimal social standing, were invited to the desert city of Yathrib to mediate between warring tribes. The name of the city, Yathrib, was later changed by Muhammad's followers to *Madinat an-Nabi* ("city of the Prophet") and later to Madina (simply meaning city; sometimes spelled Medena). Since Muhammad had worn out his welcome in Makkah, he was happy to oblige as mediator to the warring tribes. The Prophet's migration to Madina was in reality a flight, an escape, and an asylum away from the Makkan town elders who were fed up with his "new order" which threatened, as noted earlier, their political, religious, and economic power base, the very essence of their way of life. The year of his migration, or *Hijrah*, as it is known in Arabic, is so significant in Islam that the Muslim calendar begins that year, 622 A.D. Today the Islamic calendar date is always followed by the letter "H" (for *Hijrah*), which identifies it as the Islamic date and recognizes the migration of the Prophet and his followers to Madina. Followers of Islam believe that the period of time prior to the arrival and teachings of the Prophet Muhammad, with the exception of the life and times surrounding earlier prophets recognized by Muslims (such as Adam, Noah, Moses, Abraham, and Jesus), was for the most part unimportant, lost, to be minimized and marginalized, and its people were misinformed and misguided.

Over the next several years in Madina, Muhammad gained prestige and converts and had amassed a credible force, large enough that it could no longer be ignored by Makkans or anyone else. In 630 A.D. Muhammad triumphantly returned to his birth city of Makkah, demanding the destruction of all idols and receiving the recognition by the reluctant yet humbled city elders. Thus, he toppled the Makkan establishment and established his own preeminence and unquestioned political, military, social, and religious authority.

## DEFINING THE NEW RELIGION

During his years in Madina, Muhammad negotiated access to Makkah and the *Ka'bah* for his followers as the required site for an annual pilgrimage. The Prophet recognized the importance of the established pagan *Ka'bah* as a central unifying, rallying, and sacred place. However, he rejected its pagan significance and instead revealed and identified it as a place visited and even established by the Old Testament patriarch and prophet Abraham. Also, while in Madina, in order to gain the confidence and following of some of the prominent Jewish tribes, Muhammad adopted the Jewish practices of facing Jerusalem when praying, fasting on the Jewish holidays, as well as other Jewish practices. When the Jewish community of Madina rejected Muhammad, he later dropped and amended these practices, giving them a more Muslim and Arab flavor. He now called for an annual pilgrimage to Makkah instead of Jerusalem, facing Makkah when praying five times daily, and a unique Islamic month-long fast. These changes, Muslims believe, were revelations by the Angel Gabriel.

Never intending to establish a new religion, Muhammad died in 632 A.D., just ten years after his flight from Makkah. His death did not come until after he had in a relatively short time consolidated political, military, social, and religious power, and had established himself as the "Seal of the Prophets," that is, the last of God's prophets to man. As mentioned above, Muhammad and Islam accepted most Old Testament prophets, including Jesus, whom they call *Isa Bin Mariam*, or Esau son of Mary. Muhammad and Muslims accept the prophethood of Jesus, but never his deity. Islam considers the notion that God would need to have a son to be unconscionable and almost sacrilegious. Muhammad taught that God and only God should be worshiped. For this reason, Muslims have a hard time understanding and validating Christianity, especially Catholicism, when they see Catholics depicting pictures, icons, coins, and erecting and seemingly worshiping statues of central figures in their religion. I have had Muslims ask me if it is true that Christians worship idols. What Muslims see is Catholics kneeling down in front of icons, paintings, and statues of Jesus, Mary, Joseph, and the Apostles, praying to them, and even kissing their images. To Muslims it is clear: Catholics, and hence Christians, worship idols. In order to guard against falling into the practice of idol worshiping, or even its appearance, which the Prophet worked so hard to rid his people of, it is forbidden in Islam to have a painting, statue, or any graven image of Muhammad, God, or anyone, lest the image, and not God, become the object of reverence and worship.

## The Five Pillars of Islam

Muhammad left his followers with five simple prescriptions for living the life God was asking and for submitting to His will, thus becoming Muslims. These are known as the Five Pillars of Islam, to which obedience is required by all who accept Muhammad as the Seal of the Prophets. All Muslims must accept Muhammad's teachings as the inerrant word of God to mankind sent through the Angel Gabriel to the prophet of God. The Five Pillars of Islam are:

∼ Profession of Faith
∼ Prayer
∼ Almsgiving
∼ Fasting
∼ Pilgrimage to Makkah

### PROFESSION OF FAITH

This profession of faith is the simple acceptance and recitation of the statement, "*Allah* is Supreme. There is no god but *Allah*, and Muhammad is his messenger (prophet)." This rallying call was necessary early in Islam in order to distance the monotheistic teachings of Muhammad from that of the prevailing custom in Arabia of each tribe having its individual gods. This was a clear break from what was the old norm, which now distinguished it as the Prophet's new religion. By adding the second half of the profession of faith, that Muhammad is the messenger of God, it established Muhammad's authority as the Seal of the Prophets, thereby making his teachings more valid than the teachings of all prophets who preceded him and those who might come after him. Muhammad also taught that since Judaism and Christianity had already recognized the primal authority and deity of the One True God, Muslims should give Jews and Christians special favor and consideration over followers of other religions. Muhammad and Islam refer to Jews and Christians as "People of the Book," since both already possessed a sacred text of righteous and godly teaching, the Old and New Testament Scriptures.

### PRAYER

Muhammad required his followers to pray prostrate towards the city of Makkah five times per day: at daybreak, midday, midafternoon, sunset, and nightfall. Muslims are admonished to pray in a group if possible, with one person acting as the prayer leader, but alone if necessary. Muslim men and women always pray segregated in order to maintain focus of mind and ensure female modesty during prostration. Each prayer has prescribed steps, including placement of the hands, statements of the Supremacy of God, and the number of prostrations. Prior to prayer, believers are required to wash their arms up to the elbows, their feet to the ankles, and their faces with water, a ritual cleansing known as ablution. In the absence of water, they are to either use sand or simply pantomime, or go through the motion of the ablution ritual. Remember, until relatively recently, Arabia, the birthplace of Islam, was a harsh environment with precious little water to waste. Water was more essential for survival than for cleansing.

When the *Mu'azzin*, or crier, calls the faithful to prayer, he calls out, "*Allahu Akbar.*" This call to prayer, or battle cry as it is sometimes used, is a simple statement by Muslims of the omnipotence and supremacy of God. It is often translated into English as "God is Great." The simple translation "God is Great" is at a minimum an incorrect translation of the Arabic in its *Quranic* context; however, in certain contexts, the Arabic word *Akbar* can mean simply "great." What is most important for the Western reader to understand is that the translation "God is Great" does not capture the essence and strength of the *Quranic* Arabic context in this case. The Arabic word for "great" is *atheem*; a word that is not even included in the call to prayer. The translation of the word *Akbar* to "great" does not capture the full and true meaning of the Arabic word *Akbar* in its Islamic context as it attempts to identify the awesome nature of God. The word *Akbar* in Arabic is both the comparative and the superlative for "big," whereas the weak English translation of "great" is the simple declarative. A more accurate translation that captures the Islamic essence of the word *Akbar* in its true religious context is "God is Omnipotent" or "God is

Supreme." The concept of *Akbar* in Arabic intimates God's supremacy over all. The simple English translation "God is Great" leaves its meaning totally undervalued and under-translated. The complete call to prayer by the *Mu'azzin* is: "God is Supreme. There is no god but *Allah*, and Muhammad is the messenger of *Allah*. Come to prayer." This call to prayer is delivered a cappella by one man via a loud-speaker from the minaret of every mosque, in a sing-song or chanting manner, in every Muslim town and city from the Atlantic Ocean to China, five times every day.

## Almsgiving

The Prophet Muhammad emphasized giving assistance to those less fortunate, the poor, the orphaned, and generally, society's forgotten. Muhammad started out as an orphan with much less than many. He no doubt remembered the generosity of others in his behalf, even if they were extended family. Almsgiving is therefore a social prescription required by all Muslims. It is one of those easy and necessary duties one can do to improve on his ledger of good and evil, which is kept in heaven for the Judgment Day.

## Fasting

Muhammad directed his followers to fast, with no food or drink, not even water, during daylight hours for the entire month of Ramadan, the ninth lunar month. In addition to fasting for the entire month, Muslims may not take over-the-counter medication for minor ailments, discomfort or inconvenience, such as aspirin or temporary heartburn medication. They are also prohibited from smoking or engaging in sex during daylight hours. However, after sunset all activities are permitted. Exceptions from this strict regimen of fasting are made for the very young whose bodies are still developing, for the seriously ill who are under a physician's care and require prescription medication or sustenance for survival, for pregnant or nursing mothers, and for menstruating women. However, adults who miss fast days for any of the above reasons are expected and obligated to make them up after their conditions improve.

❋

## PILGRIMAGE TO MAKKAH

All able-bodied and financially capable Muslims are required to make at least one pilgrimage to Islam's birthplace, Makkah, during their lifetime. In pre-Islamic days, there was a pagan requirement for an annual pilgrimage to Makkah, which Muhammad retained. The annual pilgrimage later proved impractical because of the long distances involved as the nation of Islam grew to the far reaches of the globe, from Spain to Siam. During the pilgrimage, specific elaborate rituals of purification, prayer, circumambulating the *Ka'bah* seven times, and a ceremony of symbolically throwing stones at the devil take place in and around the city of Makkah. Upon arriving in Makkah, all pilgrims attire themselves in white as a symbol of purity, unity, and equality under God. This is a time for personal penance and prayer. After one has made the pilgrimage, he or she can add the prefix title of *Haj* or *Hajah* to his or her name, respectively, indicating they have made the *Haj*, or pilgrimage. It is considered the highest honor to have made the pilgrimage to Makkah.

❋

## THE CHARACTER OF ISLAM

Islam maintains that there are ninety-nine names for God (see Appendix D). While Muslims affirm these to be individual names for God, in reality they are more accurately attributes of God such as Omnipotent, Judge, Mighty, Creator, Merciful, Compassionate, Forgiving, Everlasting, Most Generous, to name a few. Muhammad and Islam stressed the everlastingness of God, the fear of the Judgment Day, and the mystical nature of God. For this reason when Muslims speak of God, Muhammad, and the teachings of the *Qur'an*, they do so with mystical awe, fear, and reverence. The words of the *Qur'an* are considered sacred, for they are the exact utterances of *Allah*, God. Its verses are recited with hallowed reverence and mystery. The *Qur'an's* dictates are to be accepted as the unquestioned canon word of God. A belief in the supreme Deity of *Allah*, God, is basic. Anyone who might profess to be an atheist or an agnostic would be better served not sharing this unbelief with a Muslim. The atheist's and agnostic's credibility in all areas, personal and professional, would be minimized and even totally discounted. No business transaction or time of day would be lost on someone who does not acknowledge and fear *Allah*, God. In Muslim and Arab society, even the most secular person dares not speak irreverently of God, the *Qur'an*, or the teachings of Islam, lest they blaspheme and evoke the immediate vengeance of God or be banished to everlasting hell.

## THE SPREAD OF ISLAM AND ARABISM

Following the death of the Prophet Muhammad in 632 A.D., Muslim Arab armies quickly attacked and conquered all the Near East, Middle East, and North Africa, gaining converts and soldiers as they went. Islamized far North Africans, called Berbers, were eager warriors and were in it for the adventure, power, and booty (much like the crusaders some four centuries later). One exceptionally successful Berber warrior, General *Tariq*, crossed the narrow North African straits into Spain (Europe), and continued into the Spanish interior, seizing Cordoba and Toledo for Islam. To this day, the rock gateway to Europe bears his name (Chapter 1, "Arab Identity"), *Jabal Tariq*, or Gibraltar, meaning "The Mountain of *Tariq*." Cordoba became the Arab capital of Spain where Arabs ruled from 756 until 1031 A.D., nearly three hundred years. Total Arab-Islamic influence in Spain lasted much longer, from about 709 A.D. when Berbers first entered Spain, until 1492, roughly eight hundred years, when Spanish Christian armies reconquered Granada from Muslim Arab rule for the last time.

By 718 A.D., most of the Iberian Peninsula was in Muslim Arab hands. Muslim armies attempted to penetrate farther into Western Europe and might have succeeded, but were stopped in 732 A.D. in France by Charles Martel at the Battle of Tours. This enormous conquest and occupation of a large section of the world, from Persia on the East to all the Middle and Near East, across North Africa and into Southwestern Europe to Spain, were all accomplished within one hundred years of the death of Islam's founder and prophet. One has to wonder about the course of history had Muslim Arab armies succeeded in occupying all of Europe. What languages would Europe be speaking today? What religion would be the dominant religion of Europe? In whose name would European explorers have discovered the New World (America)? What would be the dominant language and religion of North America and by inference, what would be the dominant international language of business, industry, and technology today? Regardless of what did or did not happen, Islam's conquest was impressive by any standard. What started out as voices in the desert continues to echo from minarets and capitals across the world, from Morocco to Mongolia, spreading with it the religion, language, and culture of the Arabian Desert and its people.

# Ten

# The Israel Factor

### THE FRIEND OF MY ENEMY IS MY ENEMY

In Chapter 7, "Doing Business in the Arab World," we briefly discussed the fundamental Arab principle "A friend of my friend is my friend," and its corollary, "A friend of my enemy is my enemy," with their roots in the desert culture. This is such an important aspect of Arab culture, with its international and cross-national implications, that it warrants further inquiry and amplification. No thorough discussion or understanding of Arab culture and society could be complete without a review of this principle and how it applies to Arab feelings toward Israel, and in turn, how these feelings affect Arab relations with the world.

This principle is clearly demonstrated by how the Arabs feel toward Israel and Israel's supporters. To Arabs, Israel is the enemy because Israel exists today on what Arabs consider to be stolen Arab land. There is an almost daily cry for arms from across the Muslim and Arab world to attack Israel and its supporters. The cry usually comes from Islamic extremists and radical voices such as the Saudi multimillionaire Usama Bin Ladin, who has declared holy war and issued a *Fatwa*, or religious decree, for all Muslims to kill Zionists and crusaders anywhere in the world, be they military or civilian. (In reality, since Bin Ladin is not an Islamic cleric, he is not qualified, nor does he have the religious authority, to issue a religious decree, but that has not stopped him nor deterred his followers.) The Crusader reference in the *Fatwa* is to Westerners, principally Americans and Britons, and the Zionist reference is to Israel and Israel's worldwide Jewish supporters. It is difficult for many Americans to understand and accept that people such as Usama Bin Ladin are still fighting the Crusades which ended over eight hundred years ago. Others who call for military action against Israel and its supporters are dictators such as Iraq's Saddam Hussein and Libya's Muammar al-Qadhafi, and those who have lost land to Israel in the numerous recent wars, such as Syria. Saddam Hussein's reasons are a battle cry to deflect attention from himself and his atrocities against his own people and other Arab countries (Kurds, Shiites, and Kuwaitis), and to focus attention on a pan-Arab rallying issue, opposition to Israel and Zionism. Although today most mainstream Arab leaders no longer call for Israel's destruction and have more or less accepted Israel's reality as factual, most Arabs harbor ill feelings toward Israel and would not shed a tear if Israel were destroyed militarily and completely annihilated. To date, the only Arab League countries to recognize Israel diplomatically are Egypt, Jordan, and Mauritania; however, the Arabian Gulf countries of Oman and Qatar have established Israeli trade offices. To fully understand how deep this issue of Arab-Israeli animosity is, the following review of the region's ancient and recent history is essential.

❀

## ROOTS

So the story goes, as accepted by both Arabs (Muslims and Christians) and Israelis (Jews), nearly four thousand years ago, Abram (later renamed Abraham) was a righteous man living in the land of Ur, roughly the area occupied today by the country of Iraq. One day God appeared to Abram, who was a rare monotheist of his day, believing only in the one true God among polytheists and idolaters. God told Abram to pick up his family and travel to a land God would show him, which would become Abram's and his future children's inheritance. God also promised to make Abram's descendants as numerous as the sands of the seas and the stars in the heavens. Obeying God's command, Abram, then seventy-five years old, left Ur together with his wife Sarai (later renamed Sarah), his nephew Lot, and their respective families, slaves, and servants, and traveled west. They arrived at a coastal land at the eastern end of the Mediterranean Sea in what was then the land of Canaan, inhabited by a people known as Canaanites. The fact that the land was inhabited by another people at the time Abram was to live on it and eventually inherit it did not seem to matter much to either God, Abram, or the modern day descendants of Abraham, who live by the story as proof of their rightful ownership to this land. Believers accept the story at face value as just and final since God so commanded it, with little regard to its later historical ramifications. The region Abram settled in was most likely sparsely inhabited by a people not too unlike the newly arrived Abram and his tribe, some town dwellers and some nomads. Some of the inhabitants of Canaan were undoubtedly migrating herdspeople, much like the fast-disappearing Arab Bedouin tribes of today. After arriving in Canaan, Abram and his people roamed the region looking for the most fertile lands to feed and water their herds, as Bedouins do today and have done for centuries. Although some Canaanites lived in settled towns around 1900 B.C. (nearly four thousand years ago), boundaries between settled "nations" and people were less well defined and borders more porous and fluid than they are today.

As Abram settled into his new land, he most likely lived as a wealthy owner of herds of sheep, goats, and camels, and owned numerous slaves as well. One day Sarai, Abram's wife, came to him and reminded him of God's promise to make him the "father of a great nation." The only problem was that Sarai was apparently barren and could not bear Abram children, and therefore heirs to God's covenant, since she was over ninety years old and well past the normal childbearing years. To solve the problem and help her husband, Sarai suggested to Abram that he take her Egyptian handmaid (slave), Hagar, so that he, Abram, could have children by her, and thus fulfill God's promise and begin building his "great nation." Abram, being the dutiful, obedient husband that he was, agreed to his wife's suggestion and the Bible records that "he took Hagar as a wife." Hagar then bore Abram his first son, whom they called Yishmael/Ismaeel (Hebrew and Arabic, respectively) for Ishmael, translated as "God hears."

The story gets more complicated when two more very important events take place. First, Sarai gets jealous of Hagar who apparently taunted her mistress with her ability to bear Abram a son. Sarai convinced Abram to evict Hagar and her son Ishmael from Abram's community and banish them to the desert. Hagar and Ishmael's travels and travails are less clear after this point, but God promises to care for them and not forsake them. The important historical point here is that Arabs trace their ancestry to Abram through his first son Ishmael, son of Hagar. The second important event is that Sarai has a conversation with an angel of God in which he tells her she will become pregnant and deliver a son to Abram. Sarai laughs at the angel because she is by this time in her nineties and well past the childbearing years even if she were not barren. Besides, Abram is well over one hundred years old now. According to the story, Sarai truly does become pregnant and bears a son and calls him YitsHaq, or Isaac, which translates to "he laughs" because Abram laughed at the angel when he told him Sarai would bear him a son. The important historical point here is that the Hebrews, Jews, Israelites, and modern day Israelis trace their ancestry to Abram through Isaac, son of Sarai. At this point the angel of the Lord changes Sarai's name to Sarah, and Abram's name to Abraham, meaning "father of many."

## SONS OF ABRAHAM INHERITANCE QUARREL

Today's Arabs and Jews, whoever they have become racially after centuries of wandering, occupation by numerous foreign armies, interracial and cross-ethnic marriage across a diverse gene pool of humanity, both trace their ancestry and lineage to their mutual patriarch Abraham; the Arabs through Ishmael and Hagar his mother, and the Jews through Isaac and Sarah his mother. The problem in modern times is that both factions of Abraham's line, Arabs and Jews, claim the area we know today as Palestine, as theirs by birthright of inheritance from Abraham, as promised to him and his descendants by God. The Jews argue that the covenant choosing Abraham as a righteous man and granting him the land of Canaan (Palestine/Israel) was made between God, Abraham and his then-wife Sarah, and later their child Isaac and his descendants, the Jews. Arabs claim that it was not uncommon for men in Abraham's time to have more than one wife, and Sarah was only one of Abraham's several wives. As we have seen in Chapter 9, "Islam," Muslims today are still allowed to have up to four wives, so having more than one wife is not unusual to Arabs or Muslims. Muslims continue their case by arguing that since Ishmael was Abraham's first-born son, the rightful inheritance of the land God promised Abraham belonged to Ishmael and his descendants, the Arabs. In much of the world, both in the time of Abraham and today, the lion's share of an inheritance, the birthright, is passed to the eldest son; in this case, clearly Ishmael, assuming one considers Abraham to have been legally married to Ishmael's mother, Hagar.

❈

## HEBREWS, ROMANS, AND THE DIASPORA

Approximately two thousand years had passed since the time Abraham first set foot in the Promised Land of Canaan and the time when his descendents, the Hebrews, had multiplied in sufficient numbers to take over the land from its Canaanite inhabitants. Much had happened in the meantime to the Hebrews, including their Egyptian captivity and enslavement, their emergence as a distinct unified people, and their subsequent return by Moses to the Promised Land. Scholars conclude that it was during their Egyptian captivity and pharaonic servitude that the Hebrews (later known as Jews) came together as a unified people. Around 900 B.C., or about three thousand years ago, King David established the Hebrew kingdom of Judah in southern Palestine and made the city of Jerusalem his capital. At the same time, another Hebrew kingdom was established in northern Palestine, known as the Kingdom of Israel. What is often minimized and almost never considered is that in order to establish the Hebrew kingdoms in someone else's lands, existing distinct people (such as Canaanites, Philistines, and Jebusites), together with their national aspirations and cultural identities, had to be subdued, displaced, and replaced. Jerusalem, for example, prior to King David's making it his Judean capital, belonged to the Jebusites, and was the Jebusite capital known as *Jebus-salem,* which evolved into the Hebrew name Yerushalaem; hence, the English spelling and pronunciation, Jerusalem.

In the late first century B.C., about two thousand years ago, the Romans became the Western world's superpower and occupied Palestine (as they called it), the land of the Hebrews (Jews). Roman rule was for the most part tolerant and allowed the people it conquered to exercise self-rule as long as they obeyed a few simple rules, such as paying taxes to Rome and acknowledging Roman emperors as gods. This was a bit much for the independent-minded monotheistic Jews, whose first commandment was to not worship any other god than the one true God, and who also had trouble giving tribute to anyone but God. Conflict was inevitable. The Jews became such an irritant to the Roman rulers that Rome saw it necessary to attack the Jewish capital of Jerusalem and declare all-out war on Jewish rule in what had been the Jewish homeland for some two thousand years. In the face of the attacking and now angry Romans, Jews fled Jerusalem, dispersed to the surrounding lands, and later scattered to Europe, Africa, Asia, and beyond. This dispersion is known in Jewish history as the Diaspora, lasting approximately two thousand years, from the year 70 A.D. until the end of the twentieth century.

## ZIONISM AND ARAB NATIONALISM

In the late nineteenth century, just over one hundred years ago, Jews in Europe began to seriously consider doing something about their misfortune through history as wanderers in other people's lands and their mistreatment by their various hosts. Wherever they settled in the Diaspora, Jews were blamed for all their host's ills, and vengeance was taken out on them as being the source of their host's misfortunes. The Spanish Inquisition is but one of the great tragedies of the Jewish Diaspora. Jews began to realize that unless they lived independently and ruled themselves in their own land, they would continue to be the scapegoat of the world's troubles wherever they lived. This idea of Jewish self-rule began as a dream for the Jews scattered by the Romans nearly two thousand years earlier, to reconstitute themselves in their ancestral biblical homeland of Samaria, Judea, Jerusalem, and all of Zion. The movement became known as Zionism. There was only one problem: the land of Zion (Palestine) was at this point inhabited by a people calling themselves Arabs. These Arabs, known regionally as Palestinian-Arabs because they lived in Palestine, were descendants of many different peoples who lived in and ruled this ancient land over thousands of years. The last influential invaders to have left their enduring mark on this land were the Muslim Arabs who militarily subdued and occupied the land and its people around 633 A.D., almost fourteen centuries ago. These Muslim Arabs brought with them their language, religion, and culture in the seventh century, or about fourteen hundred years ago. In time, the inhabitants of this land, Palestine, became Arabized and began thinking of themselves and referring to themselves as Arabs, specifically, Palestinian-Arabs.

In the late nineteenth century, Palestine and its Palestinian-Arab inhabitants were ruled by the Ottoman Turkish Empire. During World War I, the British forces, with the help of Arab tribes, defeated the Ottoman Turks and replaced Ottoman rule in the region with British rule. To entice and unite the otherwise independent-minded Arabs to help fight and rid Arab lands of the Ottoman Turks, Great Britain promised the Arabs that once victorious over the Turks, Arabs would be free to establish self-rule and nationhood in the newly liberated Arab lands. For the most part this came about, but not complete independence. Countries and boundaries were demarcated and such countries as Saudi Arabia, Yemen, Iraq, Syria, Lebanon, and Trans-Jordan (later called simply Jordan) were created more or less independent, but often with strings attached to Mother England. Great Britain and France carved out spheres of influence, and in effect replaced Ottoman rule with their own rule known as protectorates, or spheres of influence in Lebanon, Syria, Trans-Jordan, Palestine, Egypt, Yemen, and the Arabian Gulf states.

## HISTORICAL WATER UNDER A LAND
## BRIDGE CALLED PALESTINE

Palestine, the focus of the modern Arab-Israeli dispute, was a unique situation. Shortly after Great Britain conquered and occupied Palestine from the Ottoman Turks with the help of the Arabs, Zionist leaders persuaded the then-British Foreign Secretary, Lord Balfour, to agree "to establish a Jewish homeland in Palestine." This is the first part of what has become known as the famous (or infamous, depending on one's political perspective of the Arab-Israeli conflict) "Balfour Declaration." The second part of the sentence reads ". . . it being clearly understood that nothing shall be done which may prejudice the civil and religious rights of existing non-Jewish communities in Palestine." While the promise to establish a Jewish homeland in Palestine might have been great news for Jews of the Diaspora, Great Britain had also made earlier promises to Arab leaders in the McMahon-Sharif Hussein Correspondence regarding the establishment of new autonomous Arab countries in lands inhabited by Arabs and previously ruled by the Ottomans. British double-talk resulted in future Middle Eastern conflicts. While speaking out of both sides of its mouth to Arabs and Jews, Great Britain had also secretly agreed with France to carve up the Middle East into British and French regions of influence in the Sykes-Picot Agreement.

Unfortunately for the indigenous Palestinian-Arabs, who were the overwhelming majority of the population of Palestine, Jews and Zionists around the world were only interested in, and only paid attention to, the first part of the Balfour Declaration. The first part of the declaration is all the Zionists needed to energize their movement and mobilize Jews from around the world to return to their biblical homeland after nearly two thousand years of Diaspora. Jews began immigrating to Palestine by the thousands from all parts of the world. The only problem was the Palestinian-Arabs now living in Palestine where the Jews hoped to make their new country also had nationalistic aspirations, and were hoping to become a self-governing autonomous nation, as other Arabs were doing in newly carved-out Arab lands.

As Jews poured into tiny Palestine (about the size of the state of New Jersey), Arabs not only became suspicious and regarded the Jews as European invaders and occupiers, they also attempted to discourage the new immigrants and those who might follow them by attacking their settlements. To defend against Arab attacks, the Jewish communities built up the security of their settlements and counter-attacked Arab villages and towns. As more Jews came into the country, the attacks and counter-attacks became more frequent and bloodier. In an attempt to partially appease the Arabs, Great Britain placed a quota on the numbers of Jews who could legally immigrate into Palestine. To get around this quota, Jewish immigration organizers developed an underground that would illegally smuggle their people into Palestine. With their two-sided policy of trying to live up to promises made to both Arabs and Jews, Great Britain evoked the ire of both sides, and British soldiers became the subjects of hatred and attack by both Arabs and Jews. The situation had become so difficult, costly, and intolerable for Great Britain that it handed over the "Palestinian Problem" to the United Nations, agreeing to abide by whatever solution the United Nations could come up with for Palestine.

By this time, a somewhat seemingly unrelated event, World War II, was taking place in Europe, and the Jews once again found themselves the victims of hatred, persecution, and attempted genocide, this time at the hands of the Nazis. This desperate situation only accelerated the tempo and urgency to evacuate Jews from Europe and bring them to Palestine, where they would eventually be safe in their own homeland as promised by their Jewish leaders and the current occupiers and military rulers of the land, Great Britain.

## POINT-COUNTERPOINT

As World War II ended, the world community of nations was feeling increasingly sympathetic toward the plight of the Jews at the hands of the Nazis, and the mood was favorable in the United Nations to solve the "Jewish Problem" once and for all. The international body decided to partition Palestine into separate Arab and Jewish states along population lines as the only viable solution. The Jews accepted the plan as immediately as the Arabs rejected it. To the Jews, something from nothing was something. To the Arabs, all of Palestine was theirs, and no one nor any entity had the right to give away its land to another people. As Arabs often state their position, it is very sad what Hitler and the Nazis did to the Jews in Europe, but why make the Arabs in Palestine pay for the sins of the Nazis? Not one Arab, they continue, was ever responsible for putting even one Jew in a concentration camp, gas chamber, or an oven. It is not fair, Arabs contend, to solve the problem of people, the Jews, at the expense of another people, the Palestinian-Arabs. What kind of sense does it make, Arabs argue, to take half of

Palestine, which is Arab land, and give it to the foreign Jews from Europe, simply because they were victims of a tyrant in Europe? Arabs contend that the European tyrant should pay, not the innocent Palestinians. Of course, to the Jews no other place on earth but Palestine, their biblical homeland, would do. The United Nations actually considered making a homeland for the Jews in several other places, including Uganda and Argentina. The Jews rejected these options quickly as having no historical basis or relevance for them as a people. The Jewish ancestral homeland was in Palestine, and no other option would be considered or accepted.

Arabs reject the Jewish argument that this land, now Palestine, was given exclusively to the Jews by God through the Jewish Patriarch, Abraham. Arabs agree that the land was given to Abraham and his descendants by God, but as discussed earlier, they point out that they, the descendants of Abraham's eldest son Ishmael, are due the birthright and are the rightful inheritors of Abraham's wealth and land. The Jews counter that the promise of this land was made between God, Abraham, and Sarah; not between God, Abraham, Hagar the Egyptian servant girl, and her son Ishmael.

Arabs respond to the argument regarding Jewish and Zionists' rights to legally return to and claim land which their ancestors lived in two thousand years earlier by contending that if every people returned to where their ancestors lived at some distant point in history, then no one today would be allowed to live in the land they currently occupy. A lot of historical water has flowed underneath the land bridge of Palestine, and many people have occupied and claimed Palestine as their own since Hebrews/Jews engaged in self-rule in the region two to three thousand years earlier. Arabs will argue that if the right of return to one's ancestral land is a valid rule of international law, then, for example, all the nonnative inhabitants of the United States today who came from every continent of the world must leave and return to their original countries. Not even the so-called "Native

Americans" could remain living in America if the Jewish argument over Palestine were valid, because Native American ancestors also migrated from Siberia to the New World across Alaska and down the North American continent at the end of the last Ice Age, when North America was connected to Siberia by a frozen land bridge. Arabs assert that this argument of legitimate ownership or right to Palestine, because Jewish ancestors once lived and ruled the land, is baseless and invalid and would never stand the test of international law.

## PALESTINIAN REFUGEES: THE NEW DIASPORA

Both out of fear for themselves and their families, and in the face of fierce fighting, Palestinian-Arabs by the hundreds of thousands either left voluntarily or were forced to leave their homes, farms, property, wealth, and lives in Palestine, as the Jewish State declared its independence in April 1948. As mentioned earlier, since the Arabs rejected the United Nations Partition Plan for Palestine, no Palestinian-Arab country was ever formed. In retrospect, some Palestinians have said that they should have accepted the 1947 United Nations Partition Plan for similar reason made by the Jews: "something from nothing is something." As a result of refusing the United Nations Partition Plan of 1947, Palestinian-Arabs now have nothing. (Of note was another offer made as late as January 2001 by the Israeli government of Prime Minister Ehud Barak who offered the Palestinians much of the West Bank of the Jordan River, the Gaza strip, and East Jerusalem including the Temple Mount area. The Palestinians again rejected the offer because they thought it did not go far enough.) Palestinian-Arabs were encouraged to leave their homes and lands by numerous Arab leaders who promised to declare war on the new Jewish State and "run the Jews into the ocean." These Arab leaders promised the Palestinian-Arabs they would be returned to their homes and land in two weeks. In reality, five Arab states declared war on Israel in April 1948: Lebanon, Syria,

Jordan, Iraq, and Egypt. After one year of fighting, Israel and its Arab enemies signed an armistice agreement, which was nothing more than a cease-fire. The agreement more or less recognized Israeli rule in the lands it occupied at the signing of the armistice. The armistice was not a peace treaty, and the Arabs considered themselves to be at a continuous state of war with Israel, vowing to pick up the fight at a future date.

During this year of fighting, Israel held on to and increased the land originally given to it by the United Nations Partition Plan for Palestine. The Arabs refused to accept Israel's right of ownership of "Occupied Palestine," as they called it. In the meantime, the war had dislodged and dislocated approximately one million Palestinian-Arabs who were now living in Palestinian refugee camps, supported, housed, clothed, fed, and their children educated by the United Nations in the surrounding Arab countries of Egypt (the Gaza Strip), Lebanon, Syria, and Jordan. To this day, these Palestinian refugees and their third generation descendents continue to live in humiliating squalor and poverty in these refugee camps. Three subsequent Arab-Israeli Wars (1956, 1967, and 1973) have swelled the numbers of these refugees to over 1½ million people. Some of the displaced Palestinians with resources and education left these refugee camps, when it became obvious they would not soon be returning to Palestine, and migrated to other Arab countries as well as to Europe and the United States. However, the vast majority of these Palestinian refugees continue to live in camps after more than fifty years of the Palestinian Diaspora.

The government of Israel has refused to allow these refugees to return to their homes and lands after more than fifty years, and the Arab world for the most part refuses to absorb them and give them citizenship. Israel contends that these Palestinians left on their own accord with the hope that the combined Arab armies would destroy Israel, despite Israeli calls for them to remain in their homes. Israel argues that Arab countries with their vast territories could and should have absorbed their fellow Arabs, as Israel has absorbed several million Diaspora Jews. Arabs counterargue that Palestinian-Arabs did not leave voluntarily from Palestine, but were forced out of their homes at the end of an Israeli gun barrel. To give these Palestinian-Arabs citizenship in other Arab countries, they continue, would not solve the problem and would not achieve the goal of returning them to their rightful homeland, Palestine. Besides, they add, to give them Lebanese, Syrian, Jordanian, or Egyptian citizenship would strip them of their Palestinian national identity. Israelis argue that Arabs are deliberately not solving the Palestinian problem by refusing to absorb the refugees because, in so doing, the "problem" would go away and the Arabs would not have a pan-Arab rallying cause nor an issue of contention with Israel.

Arabs compare the Palestinian plight of 1948 to that of the Serbian ethnic cleansing attempt of ethnic Albanians from Kosovo in 1999. In both cases, they claim, Muslims were evicted from their homes; in 1948 Muslims were evicted by Jewish Israelis in Palestine, and in 1999 Muslims were evicted by Christian Serbs in Kosovo. Arabs argue that the only difference between the Palestinian refugee problem of 1948 and the ethnic Albanian problem of 1999 is that in 1999 the world had CNN to record, inform, outrage, and mobilize public action against a grave injustice and a human tragedy. Arabs conclude that, unfortunately for them, no such medium was available when Palestinian-Arabs were losing their homes and forced into becoming refugees.

## THE FRIEND OF MY ENEMY IS MY ENEMY

Arabs consider Jewish ownership and unilateral rule of Palestine to be not only baseless and wrong, but also consider the Jews to have stolen Palestine from them. Arabs across the entire world today view Jews, Zionists, and Israelis to be their collective enemy and the single unifying cause on which they all agree. Arabs extend the enemy list to anyone, any nation, or any power which helps Israel maintain its rule over, and occupation of, Palestine and the Palestinian people. The ultimate insult to Arabs is Israel's complete autonomy and rule over Jerusalem, considered to be Islam's third-most holy city after Makkah and Madina, a situation which evokes deeply rooted enmity and belligerency in the Arab and Muslim world.

Arabs sometimes see the United States as duplicitous when, on the one hand, it says it wants to be a friend of the Arabs, and yet on the other hand, whenever there is a United States presidential election every candidate always pledges to support and maintain Israel's military superiority over the Arabs. Arabs also point out how the United States agrees to sell or give Israel the latest variant fighter aircraft and every state-of-the-art weapon and missile it could carry, with which Israel has free reign to use against all Arab adversaries. However, Arabs observe that when they ask the United States to purchase a similar weapon system, the United States Congress, empowered by Israeli lobby reelection dollars, produces a plethora of obstacles, restrictions, and limitations, making the sale an impossibility. Rather than grovel and endure the humiliation of being refused, the Arab militaries often do their military shopping elsewhere (usually France and sometimes England and Russia), where they perceive a more evenhanded approach, and where they believe they can buy comparable state-of-the-art weaponry.

In this regard, Arabs see the United States as a modern day Great Britain who spoke out of both sides of its mouth about sovereignty in Palestine before, during, and after World War I. How, the Arabs ask today, can the United States claim to be interested in Arab issues when it supports what the Arabs consider to be their unanimously agreed-upon number one enemy? Arabs assert that the only reason the United States and the West show any interest in Arab issues is because of the availability of oil under Arab sands. They add that if it were not for oil, and if the oil ran out tomorrow, the United States and the West would not give the Arabs the time of day. As a result of this perceived double standard by the West, terrorist groups have emerged in the Muslim and Arab world to attack what they believe to be enemies of the Arabs and Muslims, from which we hear cries by the likes of Usama Bin Ladin to attack Jews and crusaders, their euphemism for Israel and its Western supporters. As a result of the perceived blind support of Israel by the West, Arabs come away with the unshakable and powerful conclusion, "The friend of my enemy is my enemy."

It is imperative that the reader understand this element of the Arab equation as he attempts to deal with the Arab, for it is ever present in the heart of the Arab as he deals with the Westerner. To Arabs, American and Western favoritism of Israel is at Arab expense. Arabs accuse the West, particularly the United States, of a double standard, unfair treatment, and an uneven playing field when it comes to dealing with Arab states and Israel. The Israel factor is a wedge between Arabs and the West, America in particular, which must be resolved if there is to be complete and unencumbered dialogue, openness, acceptance, and sincere friendship between the Arab world and the West. As long as the Palestinian-Israeli issue is outstanding and unresolved, it will be the single biggest obstacle preventing a genuine Middle East-West understanding.

# Eleven

# Arab Perceptions of Americans

### REAL AMERICANS

At times, Arabs have a conveniently narrow view of who Americans are. This points to an Arab identification bias regarding people's true identity. Unfortunately, in the case of Americans, and Westerners in general, Arabs are only partially correct. When Arabs think of Americans, they think of and refer to real Americans as white, normally of Anglo or at least European descent, and Christian. They conveniently ignore the millions of nonwhite Americans, who are soon to become the majority, who make up the vast American heritage and diversity. They do themselves and Americans a disservice with this myopic stereotyping. Proof of this bias is found in the following Arab words and actions.

### U.S. NAVY SHOOTDOWN

In 1983, during the United States military involvement in Lebanon's Civil War as part of the multinational truce disengagement force, an American Navy pilot was shot down over the Bekka' Valley in Lebanon. The Navy flyer, Lieutenant Goodman, was a black American. The fact that he had been bombing Arab fighters in his United States fighter warplane became conveniently discounted and immaterial to the Arabs. Because he was black, the Arabs decided he should be returned to "his people" because he was not a real American. Real Americans, Arabs reasoned, are white, Arab-hating, Israeli-loving people of European ancestry; Lieutenant Goodman, a black man, did not fit this narrow Arab view of real Americans. Arabs reasoned that black Americans, whose ancestral home of Africa is closer to the Middle East than it is to America, would never on their own accord bomb and kill Arabs. Continued to its logical conclusion, this reasoning would presumably intimate that white Americans have an innate affinity for wanting to bomb and kill Arabs, but black Americans would not. And to whom did the Lebanese captors, through their Syrian overlords, release this Arab-killing, but not-so-real black American man? They released him to that other not-so-real American Jesse Jackson. In so doing, Arabs were saying to the people they perceived to be the real Americans (whites): To show our displeasure with your action of killing Arabs, instead of keeping him prisoner, we release him to his people because he was surely duped into attacking Arabs by his "white masters," and he and his people are, like Arabs, oppressed and discriminated against by real (white) Americans. By releasing this black aviator, Arabs were somehow hoping that America's pride would be wounded and her policy toward the Middle East discredited.

At times like this, Arabs conveniently forget it was their Arab ancestors who were the first people to capture, enslave, and sell Africans as slaves, and that it was Arab traders in North and East Africa who sold the first black African slaves to other Arabs and later to Europeans. When we look at the Arab world today, specifically the Arabian Peninsula, we need to understand where black Arabs came from. Undoubtedly, some of their ancestors came to the Arab world as traders and stayed, but the vast majority were captured and brought to Arab lands as slaves of the Arabs.

From an American perspective, it is worthwhile to review the Navy flyer's American credentials and see whether he fits in as a fully integrated real American who has benefited from the opportunities and advantages America has to offer. Lieutenant Goodman, who, incidentally, was married to a white woman, was a university graduate, had the physical and mental "right stuff" to be accepted as a United States naval officer, was an aircraft carrier-qualified fighter pilot, and was earning well above the average American income. His credentials and background do not fit the profile of a person who deserves world sympathy as being underprivileged, oppressed, and discriminated against, or one who was not given an equal opportunity at the American dream.

## U.S. EMBASSY TAKEOVER IN IRAN

Another example, which this time involves Iranians (Persians, not Arabs) but which deals with the same standards of shortsightedness and bias against perceived real Americans, took place when Iranian Islamic revolutionaries occupied the United States Embassy in Tehran and took American citizens hostage in 1979. As Muslims, Iranians share many cultural values with Arabs, since Arab-Islamic armies also conquered and converted Iranians (Persians), as they did other countries and people throughout the Middle East, North Africa, Europe, and Asia, (as we have seen in Chapters 1 and 9, "Arab Identity" and "The Essence of Islam," respectively). Iran and Turkey are two of the larger Islamic conquered countries where the Arabic language did not take hold but where other Arab cultural values did.

As with the United States Navy flyer's release, the Iranian Islamic revolutionaries released all women (with one exception) and all nonwhite Americans shortly after overrunning the United States Embassy in Tehran. The revolutionary activists held the remaining so-called real Americans hostage for 444 days. The Iranian revolutionaries did not release these American hostages until the day Ronald Reagan took office as President of the United States. The Iranian revolutionaries released these "not-so-real American" nonwhites for the same reasons the Lebanese and Syrians released the American flyer.

They reasoned that the United States Government would surely not place in a position of trust and valued authority any of these nonwhite, not-so-real Americans, and therefore they would have little intelligence or political value as hostages.

Before leaving this topic, a further word is needed for Arabs, Middle Easterners, or any others who might have a misunderstanding of who Americans really are. Americans come from all ethnic, racial, religious, and linguistic points of the world. The means by which people came to America differ, and in some cases were brutal and shameful, but that does not mean that the descendents of any one group of American immigrants are any less American and have fewer rights than any other group. All Americans salute the same flag and are supposed to be treated equally under the law. Of course, there are exceptions and there have been far too many abuses by one group over another throughout American history, even today. The ugly exceptions notwithstanding, in the United States of America, one is free to worship as one wishes without fear of being beaten with a stick by some self-proclaimed morality god-squad.

In some Muslim countries, such as Saudi Arabia, erecting a church building is against the law, as is showing outward symbols of one's faith, such as a cross or a Star of David on a necklace. These passive acts of expressions of religious freedom will get one hauled off to jail and/or flogged on the spot, as a female would be for not covering her head in public or not wearing a long enough and conservative enough dress to suit the morality police. These differences in cultural norms and limitations on personal liberties are issues Westerners must know about before visiting and working in Arab or Muslim countries. Americans do not have to agree with or even like these Islamic limitations on individual liberties, as they know them in the West, but they do have to abide by these restrictions when traveling, working, and living in some Muslim countries, just as foreigners have to respect

American laws and norms of acceptable behavior when they are in the United States.

## REAL ARABS

Finally, Arabs also have a bias as to who they consider to be real Arabs. Christian Arabs are often singled out for suspicion in East-West issues as siding with the West over the Arab position. For example, just prior to the 1991 Persian Gulf War, a Christian Arab friend, who lived in the now predominantly Muslim Palestinian-Arab city of Nazareth, expressed his concerns for his family's safety and that of his property. He said that if the war went badly for Iraq (as a group, Palestinians supported Saddam Hussein), local Muslim Arabs (his fellow blood countrymen) might turn on him as an expression of hatred toward the West. This, he reasoned, was because Muslim Arabs see Christianity as a Western religion imported by the crusaders with all its bad blood and its history of killing Muslims. According to some Muslims, Christian Arabs, because of their religious beliefs, are more loyal to the West than to the *Ummah al-Arabiyyah*, the greater Arab Nation. This is an example of how strongly the Muslim religion impacts the everyday lives and thoughts of Muslim Arabs. The perception by some Muslim Arabs that Christianity is a Western religion may sound a bit confusing, since in reality Christianity has its roots in the Middle East (Bethlehem, Nazareth, Jerusalem, and the Galilee), and is in fact, a Middle Eastern and Asian religion just like the other two great world monotheistic religions of Judaism and Islam.

## WESTERN PERCEPTIONS

Westerners are often heard to complain that the notion of shame occurring only when someone is a witness to a social or moral taboo lends itself to hypocrisy (Chapter 3, "Shame Versus Guilt"). They also complain that although Arabs and Muslims profess to believe in a strict value system, they often act in a contrary manner when they think no one of significance (another Muslim) is watching. Westerners also observe some Arabs who come to the West and drink alcohol to the point of intoxication and others who openly carouse with women, all ostensibly forbidden by Islam. Unfortunately for Arab credibility, what Westerners see is a double standard by Muslims, and by inference, Arabs. What Westerners should remember, before becoming overly judgmental regarding Arab duplicity, is that no people of any religious conviction, be they Christians, Muslims, Jews, Buddhists, or any other religion, have a monopoly on deviating from the straight and narrow.

### WESTERN MODEL OF CRIME AND PUNISHMENT

Western society, as far back as the great Greek civilization, values and stresses the preeminence of individual rights as opposed to group rights. As presented in Chapter 2, "Social Character," Arab society values group rights at the expense of the rights of the individual. To protect the rights of the individual, the West presumes innocence until proven otherwise in a court of law, places the burden of proof on the prosecution, provides trial by a jury of one's peers, and allows for several levels of extensive appeals which are of great monetary cost to society. Only after all possibilities of doubt have been exhausted is an individual found guilty of offending society, the group.

Punishment in the West is often directed at providing the offender (the individual) a second chance through rehabilitation. The Western system of punishment is limited, temporary, and ultimately forgiving of the offender except in the most heinous crimes. In recent years American society has begun demanding what appears to be a shift toward greater punishment for the offender rather than rehabilitation for such crimes as murder. This shift more closely resembles the Arab and Old Testament model of an eye for an eye.

## ARAB MODEL OF CRIME AND PUNISHMENT

By contrast, Arab society, with its roots in desert cultural group survival concerns, moves quickly to rid itself of the offender who threatens society. In practice, guilt is presumed until proven otherwise; the burden of proof of innocence is on the accused; trial is often by a prosecuting judge, not a jury of one's peers, and trial is swift with limited or no appeal. Emphasis is on the quick removal of the threat to society, the group.

Punishment in the Arab world is quick, severe, more long lasting, more difficult from which the convicted can recover, and often permanent. Arab prison sentences are normally longer than those in the West for similar crimes. Prisons and prison conditions are much harsher than the amenities available in United States prisons, such as recreational facilities and educational opportunities which come at a price tag of $60,000 per prisoner per year. In general, Arab and Muslim criminal justice is more interested in punishment than in rehabilitation—in other words, punishment for the criminal and justice for the victim and society. Arabs, with their swift criminal justice system, are often very confused by the Western legal and criminal justice system, which they view as more justice for the criminal than for the victim and society. This is yet another example of the difference between the two societies—emphasis on the individual in the West, as opposed to the group or society in the Middle East, a by-product of the Middle Eastern desert cultural roots versus the Western concern for the individual.

## THE REAGAN SHOOTING

The attempt on the life of President Ronald Reagan in 1982 is one example of the differences between American and Arab views of crime and punishment. Arabs, in a rhetorically confused and amused manner, wonder if President Reagan's shooter had been found innocent by reason of insanity or any other reason, then are law enforcement agencies looking for the real attempted murderer who actually shot Mr. Reagan? They continue with their rhetorical question and wonder if President Reagan's shooter, whom we all saw on television and who was subdued immediately by the Secret Service, is innocent, who is the real shooter? Arabs assume that President Reagan's shooter was insane, because as they reason, anyone who shoots another person has to be "crazy." To Arabs, being "crazy" or insane does not absolve one from being held accountable for having committed a heinous crime, nor does it give society the right to excuse him of the act. In Arab society, a murderer would most certainly have to be "crazy," for as soon as he is caught, society will execute him.

There is another dimension of crime and punishment in Arab society which has no equivalent in the West. To preserve Arab values and culture, Arab society imposes more severe penalties on individual offenses than does the West and punishes certain acts which are not considered crimes in the West. Theft, for example, in its most extreme Islamic punishment, results in the amputation of the criminal's right hand after the third offense. Drug trafficking in the Arab world often receives swift capital punishment, the preferred method being beheading or firing squad, even after only the first offense. Consequently, the incidence of repeat offenders is extremely low in the Arab and Muslim world.

In defending their system of punishment, Arabs are quick to point out crime rate comparison statistics between the West and their society. For example, they point to the statistics showing the high percentage of American women who will become victims of violent crimes, including rape, while the likelihood of their Arab sisters being so victimized is almost nonexistent. Robbery in America and the West is another crime with high statistics, while in the Arab world its incidence is extremely low. Arabs, therefore, conclude that their system of punishment is superior to that of the West, and does a better job of protecting its citizens (the group). They go one step further by asserting that their culture, which includes their religious teachings and their entire value system, is superior to all others and must therefore be the correct God-chosen way of life for all mankind.

Generally speaking, one can leave one's car or home unlocked in the Arab world with valuables displayed in the open, without fear of their being stolen. Arab society has a greater respect for the personal property of others than do most other cultures. Theft, vandalism, petty indiscriminant destruction by juveniles, and defacing of public or private property are not considered as acceptable "youthful indiscretions," nor are they tolerated as excusable "boys will be boys" pranks. One could argue that petty acts of robbery and vandalism, or crime in general, are low in the Arab world because of their vast oil wealth where everyone is wealthy and everything is plentiful. This assumption is faulty on two counts. First, not all Arab countries have oil and are wealthy, such as Lebanon, Syria, Jordan, Palestine, Yemen, Egypt, Sudan, Libya, Tunisia, Algeria, and Morocco. Yet crime in these countries is not only extremely low by Western standards, but they enjoy some of the lowest crime rates in the world. Second, my experience in living and traveling among Arabs for the past fifty years is that Arab society is more respectful of the sanctity of other people's property. This may have to do with the Muslim belief that a ledger of one's deeds of good and evil is maintained by the angels for which each person will have to answer on the Judgment Day.

## AMERICA HAS LOST HER SOUL

Arabs, with horrified indignation, look in disbelief at American youth who attack, kill, and injure their fellow schoolmates in shooting rampages, or what they call the Western invention of the serial murderer. Arabs wonder what can be said about a culture, which from their perspective, allows, fosters, and breeds such unforgivable criminal activity against society (the group). Arabs have no difficulty pointing at the culprit and reasons for such wanton disregard for the sanctity of human life. They say it all started when the United States decided to go to extreme measures to separate Church (morality) from State (secularity), which ultimately resulted in State-sponsored abolition of any and all religion. They point to the American Supreme Court having removed prayer from public schools as an example of the removal of solid moral teachings, thus helping to distance society from having to answer to a higher authority. They contend that without the moral values that come from strong religious teachings and convictions, individuals lose the sense of right and wrong. Arabs say the West should return to and emphasize moral and ethical teaching, both at home and in the school, without necessarily calling it religion. America, Arabs feel, should bring back ethics, values, morality, and respect for human dignity, which only comes from a fear of God, knowing that all actions will have to be accounted for on the Judgment Day. They say America has lost not only its values, but also its direction and, most seriously, its soul.

# Twelve

# Unholy War

### Arabs, Islam, and *Jihad*

I t is with great reluctance that I write of this subject in a book dedicated to Arab cultural understanding. This book is not about terrorism or equating any culture or religious group with terrorism. However, because of several lethal attacks directed against the United States during the past decade, perpetrated by radical Middle Easterners culminating in the murderous events of September 11, 2001, at the World Trade Center in New York, the Pentagon, and in Pennsylvania, the issue needs to be addressed in order to separate fiction from fact and myth from reality.

Arabs and Muslims often complain that the West unfairly perceives and paints all Muslims and Arabs, especially Palestinians, as terrorists. Of course, this exaggerated overgeneralization is wrong and a dangerous misperception. However, the misperception of associating Arabs and/or Muslims with terrorism is fueled when Westerners see concealed camera videotape evidence of Muslim Arabs building a bomb in their New York City safe house, while in the foreground a Muslim Arab member of the terrorist cell is seen kneeling and praying in the traditional Muslim manner. This scenario occurred again most recently when the investigation revealed that members of the cell that attacked the twin towers of the World Trade Center and the Pentagon on

September 11, 2001, were not only all Arabs but also Muslims who had converted a room in one of their rented safe houses into a mosque, or prayer room. With this vivid picture in mind, it is hard for Americans to not equate one with the other (Arabs and Muslims with terrorism), which advocates the killing of Americans under the illegitimate and supposed authoritative guise of religious and nationalistic pretexts. This type of action, praying on the one hand, while building bombs and planning and executing suicide aircraft attacks on the other, is viewed by Westerners as either incompatible and inconsistent with religion as Westerners understand it, or hypocritical in the least. Westerners, especially Americans, are also left with the strong conviction that the incompatibility of violence and religion is incriminating and indicting of a people (Arabs) and their religion (Islam). They take the perpetrators of these acts at their word when they declare *Jihad* (Holy War) against "crusaders" (a euphemism for Americans) and Zionists (Jews and Israelis).

## ISLAM AND *JIHAD*

We in the West have translated the word *Jihad* into English to mean Holy War, and today much of the world has come to know the word in this vein. Unfortunately, in an attempt to quickly identify the concept and quantify it in a neat little package, we have mistranslated the concept and now have an incomplete, inadequate, and misleading understanding of the real meaning of *Jihad* in Islam. In its purist form the Arabic word *Jihad* means struggle, toil, to strive, exert, put forth effort, and diligence. It can also take on a military connotation of combat or struggle, but the word has a much broader usage than one limited to military action.

Islam discusses three types of *Jihad*. The first and most important type of *Jihad* which Muslims are to engage in is, according to Imaam Abdur-Rashid of Harlem, New York, a "struggle to purify the soul, a struggle or a striving against one's own evil inclinations." In other words, the Islamic essence of *Jihad* and its most significant purpose for being a part of the Muslim religion is to admonish Muslims to struggle, toil, strive, exert, put forth effort, and be diligent in deep soul-searching and self-purification. It is a spiritual admonition to Muslims to eject and purge the evil within one's soul and get right with God. The second stage of *Jihad*, according to Imaam Abdur-Rashid, applies to a Muslim community or nation, which is admonished "to lift your voice in the face of a tyrant on behalf of justice." This action is to be conducted by the community of Muslim believers to rid themselves of a Muslim tyrant who is ungodly and mistreating of his countrymen, contrary to the teachings of Islam. The third and final level of *Jihad*, according to Imaam Abdur-Rashid, is to struggle "for the sake of Islam and the Islamic community, or against non-Muslims." The *Quranic* reference usually cited regarding this third state of *Jihad* is ". . . and fight them on until there is no more persecution and the religion becomes *Allah's*" (*Sura*/Chapter 2:190-193). Imaam Hendi of Georgetown University has identified this reference to describe a particular situation which faced the Prophet Muhammad when he was defending the city of Medina.

The *Qur'an*, like the Christian Bible, and particularly the Jewish Holy Scriptures, the Old Testament (the *Tanakh*, sometimes called *Torah*, although the *Torah* is technically only the first five books of the Hebrew scriptures, or Pentateuch), has references to the justified use of violence condoning military action against the enemies of God. However, similar to the *Qur'an*, all such references are contextually specific referring to a particular event. Like the Bible, the *Qur'an* has far more references compelling man to show compassion, love, and kindness to his fellow man than references justifying violence. Those who choose to find *Qur'anic* references to take up arms against their fellow man can do so by taking the Scriptures out of context and can justify their hateful and murderous acts. In the Christian West, specifically the United States, from the seventeenth through the nineteenth centuries, slave owners biblically "justified" enslaving African Negroes by claiming that their black skin identified them as having the "mark of Cain" and were thus cursed by God to be slaves. Finally, like the Bible, the *Qur'an* on occasion contains contradictions which can be used by those looking to "justify" their hatred, violence, and murder.

Americans would say to Arabs and Muslims that if they do not want Americans to make a Muslim Arab terrorist link, then at the very least Arabs and Arab leaders should publicly and repeatedly condemn the terrorist acts by militant extremist Muslims and disavow any relationship between the terrorist act and Arab or Islamic society. To date, only a very few courageous Arab and Muslim leaders, such as President Husni Mubarak of Egypt and most recently President Pervez Musharraf of Pakistan, have gone on record to publicly condemn terrorism and have taken measures to outlaw and arrest extremist Muslim groups who advocate violence. The world needs to hear Arab and Muslim leaders condemn terrorist groups and acts within their countries, shut down terrorist cells, not allow them to continue to live and operate freely and safely, recruit fighters, collect money, and train their fighters. To be credible, the Arab leadership needs to condemn acts of terror with the same public relations energy they use to condemn Americans in the Arab press when they are dissatisfied with any issue of American-Middle East foreign policy, particularly as it applies to Israel. At some very basic level, the creation and the nurturing of these extremist terrorist Arab and Muslim movements is a product of the societies from which they come. When these societies do not at a minimum condemn the anti-Western and anti-American rhetoric of Islamic extremist groups within their countries, by their inaction they are condoning and nurturing them and thus giving them life and approval. I place partial blame for the success of extremist religious groups of any religion squarely on the shoulders of the leaders of the countries from which the murdering terrorists come. I also hold their governments' civil and religious leaders at least partially culpable for allowing hatred to have a nurturing environment in which to incubate and flourish.

In reality, the religion of Islam condemns the taking of innocent life. Islam makes a great distinction between killing soldiers in a war and the indiscriminant taking of human life as occurred on September 11, 2001. According to an Islamic decree issued on September 14, 2001, by Slih Bin Mohamed Al-Lahiddan, the Chairman of the Islamic Supreme Judicial Council of Saudi Arabia, specifically in response to the terrorist act of September 11, 2001:

"Aggression against those who have committed no crime and the killing of innocent people . . . are not permissible even during wars. Killing the weak, infants, women and the elderly, and destroying property are considered serious crimes in Islam. Anyone who commits such crimes are the worst of people. Aggression, injustice, and gloating over the kind of crime we have seen (in New York, Washington and Pennsylvania) are totally unacceptable and forbidden in Islam. Inflicting a collective punishment is considered by Islam as despicable aggression and perversion. Killing innocent people is by itself a grave crime, quite apart from terrorizing and committing crimes against infants and women. Such acts do no honor to he who commits them, even if he claims to be a Muslim. These sorts of crimes are pernicious."

The scholar concludes with his strongest remarks against the perpetrators of this murderous act by saying, "This barbaric act is not justified by any sane mindset or any logic; nor by the religion of Islam. This act is pernicious and shameless and evil in the extreme."

However, Americans argue that it is one thing to have official Islamic scholars condemn such acts of terrorism while radical Muslims, such as Usama Bin Ladin and others, advocate attacks on the West and the United States. What is wrong with presuming legitimacy of the likes of Usama Bin Ladin is that neither he nor other Muslim advocates of attacking the West and the United States have the religious legal authority within Islam to declare a *Fatwa* (a religious decree) or *Jihad*, as explained above. In Islam, only the clerics (Imaams, as explained in Chapter 9, "The Essence of Islam") have the legal authority to declare a *Fatwa*. Neither Bin Ladin nor any other free-lancing Muslim radical is any more a spokesperson for Islam as David Koresh or Jim Jones were spokespersons for Christianity. Bin Ladin, like Koresh and Jones, is nothing more than a cult leader and that is all. Because Bin Ladin, Koresh, and Jones had, and still have followers, certainly does not give them legitimacy or authority; it just makes them dangerous. It would be just as wrong and unfair to equate Bin Ladin and his followers with mainstream Islam or mainstream Arab thought, as it would be to equate Koresh and Jones with mainstream Christianity or American behavior.

That said, this cult figure must have some appeal within the greater Muslim and Arab community. He has hit several raw nerves within the Muslim and Arab world which has given him some followership. The nerve he has hit is, as he sees it first, his intense hatred of the secular, amoral, immoral, and perverted Western lifestyle, which he sees as ultimately threatening Arab and Muslim society (Chapter 13, "Conclusion, A Clash of Cultures"). With the "anything goes" immodesty and mentality of Western dress (primarily for women), the open display and acceptance of pornography, homosexuality, and an "in your face" amoral hedonistic lifestyle as seen in Western movies, television, and the media in general (such as the Playboy channel, Howard Stern, and X-rated movies on demand), the Bin Ladins of the Arab and Muslim world see Western society as being against everything which God and Islam teach. Bin Ladin-type Muslim extremist cults see it as their moral obligation to carry on the fight for God to prevent the spread of immorality and amorality, particularly to the Arab and Muslim world. They see the West as being the enemy of God, which therefore gives them the moral authority and legitimacy to wage their unholy war.

Bin Ladin was also at odds with his own government and country of Saudi Arabia for "getting in bed" with the "Western infidels" when Saudi Arabia allowed the United States and other foreign forces to enter Saudi territory to launch Desert Storm against Iraq. These foreigners blatantly exhibited cultural insensitivity to their host country by bringing with them different practices contrary to Islamic tradition and teachings, such as publicly allowing their women's heads to be uncovered and permitting the women to wear offensive clothing, specifically men's attire (uniforms). This behavior was considered to be extremely immodest because it revealed the shape and contours of the women's bodies. Often these warrior-women were seen dressed only in their T-shirts and uniform pants working alongside the men. They also brought with them customs unacceptable to Islam, such as eating pork and drinking alcohol, and were often loud, offensive, and disrespectful of Arab and Muslim customs, tradition, and acceptable norms of behavior. To Bin Ladin and his followers, Saudi Arabia is sacred territory, the home of the two holiest shrines of Islam in the cities of Makkah and Madina. By not only allowing these foreign forces (particularly the United States) to come into Saudi Arabia, but also permitting them to stay eleven years after the fact, Bin Ladin sees the United States as defending and preserving the "corrupt and illegitimate" Saudi government which is not following the teachings of Islam as he sees it.

The other nerve, which gave Bin Ladin and others such intense hatred of the West and particularly the United States, is what has already been discussed in great detail in Chapter 10 and elsewhere throughout this book, the Israel factor. It is impossible to overemphasize the Arab world's disdain for Israel in its midst. As has already been discussed, Israel is first seen as having stolen the Arab land of Palestine from its rightful inhabitants and owners, and the United States is seen by the Arab world as the only reason Israel retains its grip and heavy iron fist of suppression and occupation of Arab lands. Through Arab eyes, the Palestinians and the Arab world have been defeated, dishonored, and shamed at the hands of Israel in the wars of 1948, 1956, 1967, 1973, and 1982. Arab anger and hatred toward the United States are amplified by the fact that the United States has been Israel's steadfast advocate in the United Nations and in every other world forum since every United States administration beginning with President Harry Truman. As the Arabs see it, if the United States would only apply the slightest bit of pressure on Israel, Israel would not be able to maintain its hold and occupation of Palestine. But the Arabs know in their heart that the United States is unbalanced in its national policy, favoring Israel. The Arabs, and specifically the Palestinians, feel that they have no other voice, no other forum or authority where they can plead their case. They are the forgotten people and no one cares. They are desperate, and desperate people perpetrate desperate actions. The attack on the United States on September 11, 2001, had as part of its message a cry for vengeance against "the friend of my enemy." While there are many in the Arab world who regret the loss of innocent lives as a result of the September 11, 2001, suicide attacks, there are also, unfortunately, many Arabs today, who say under their breaths that America got what it deserved because of the United States' favoritism and  unbalanced policy toward Israel.

The reason the Bin Ladins of the world appeal to so many in the Muslim and Arab world is not so much that Arabs and Muslims approve of and would join in the killing of innocent Americans and Israelis, but because he and his ilk obscure their message of hatred and murder by appealing to hot-button Arab and Muslim issues. They further confuse the issue by playing the Israel card and wrapping themselves in the flag of Islam and making their message appear just. This is not unlike what Saddam Hussein of Iraq did when he invaded and occupied Kuwait in 1990 and 1991. Saddam Hussein tried deflecting attention away from his invasion and occupation of a fellow Arab and Muslim country by attempting to make it a Muslim cause when he placed the words "*Allahu Akbar*" (God is Supreme) on the Iraqi flag and by playing the Israel card. Saddam Hussein is as secular an Arab head of state as they come. He is anything but religious. However, he conveniently wears his religion on his sleeve for show as necessary. By wrapping themselves in Islam, Bin Ladin and Saddam Hussein found a following in the Muslim and Arab world on a few issues while their irrational, unbalanced, and evil megalomania core becomes obscure in the fog and smoke of half-baked truth and rhetoric.

Such are the time-proven ways of all cult figures. While spewing hatred against a specific group, sprinkled with hot-button issues with broad appeal, over time they brainwash their followers into accepting and doing almost anything asked of them. The followers of the Bin Ladins of the Muslim and Arab world have lost sight of absolute right and wrong and of the accurate teachings of their own religion. They blindly go where they are directed. Bin Ladin's hate messages often find fertile ground and appeal especially among, but are not limited to, the less educated, disenfranchised, and poorer Arab and Muslim populations. Contrary to what the Bin Ladins of the world want people to believe, it is not the West or any organized religion that has chosen to color radical Muslim Arabs' intense jealousy and hatred of the West, particularly the United States, in religious terms. Bin Ladin and Saddam Hussein and company have brought this distorted, vile, and perverted hatred to the West and have attempted to obscure its aim by labeling it a religious conflict, *Jihad*, required of all devout Muslims and Arabs. The radical religious and self-appointed Islamic extremists have sought to blame the West, specifically the United States, for all their faults, failures, and shortcomings. They have chosen to create an East-West conflict where none existed and have further distorted reality by adding the wedge of religion and "religionizing" the conflict. Let the reader be reminded that it was not the West, but Arab and Muslim extremists, zealots, and cultists who brought the fight to the West and labeled their cause a "Holy War" (*Jihad*).

# Thirteen

# Conclusion

### A Clash of Cultures

As we look at the cultural uniqueness and difference between Western and Arab cultures, we Westerners tend to compare the Arab culture to our own culture and make judgments about Arabs, as any people would when exposed to another culture. In the judging process, we make value judgments of right and wrong. Some aspects of Arab culture we find acceptable and right, while others we find unacceptable and sometimes label them as wrong. Arabs today are constantly exposed to Western culture through the entertainment media (movies and television), fashion, books, magazines, as well as personal interaction with Westerners, and evaluate the West's expressions, customs, and mores against Arab and Islamic values of acceptable and unacceptable norms of behavior. Before being too critical of Arab culture, it behooves the Western reader to examine a few oddities of Western culture that Arabs find confusing and unacceptable by their standards of right and wrong.

As Arabs look at the West, they like and accept many Western technological developments and adopt some of these advances which add to the quality of human life, such as television, telephones, air conditioning, cars, airplanes, cell phones, and computers. At the same time, Arabs observe and often reject what they consider to be negative consequences of Western society, which go against Arab and Muslim values and which they feel would degrade and erode their culture. Real world examples always make the point best.

## WESTERN PROMISCUITY AND IMMORALITY

An almost unanimous cry of repulsion and rejection is heard from across the Arab and Muslim world in reaction to Western premarital promiscuity. Arabs contend that if the promiscuity of Western youth is the price of accepting Western culture, then they categorically reject the West as evil, profane, morally bankrupt, and unacceptable and will have no part it. For this reason, we hear of countless Arab and Muslim fathers kidnapping their young children, especially daughters, from their Western mothers, returning them to the Muslim Arab world in order to remove them from what they perceive to be the evil, decadent, and profane Western lifestyle. I personally know several Muslim and Christian Arab families who, after immigrating to the West for economic or political reasons, returned to their Arab country of birth just prior to their daughters reaching the age of puberty.

The major reasons Arabs reject Western society and why they have difficulty embracing the West, or casting their lots totally in the Western camp, is what they consider to be Western duplicity and moral decay. Throughout this book we have examined some of these aspects within specific Arab contexts. The following is a review of specific negative aspects of Western and American culture as seen through Arab and Muslim eyes. These aspects of Western life are issues that Arab and Muslim societies point to with indignation as unacceptable and incompatible with their culture and are a big part of why Arab and Muslim societies fear Western cultural influences on their culture.

~ THE ISRAEL FACTOR: Arabs summarize this point by asking, "How can I be the friend of the friend of my enemy?" This position is an inconsistent and irreconcilable concept to Arabs (Chapter 10, "The Israel Factor"). The Israel factor is at the top of the Arab list of why they believe the United States cannot be considered to be a true friend of the Arab world and is at the core of the Arab and Muslim world's contention with the West in general and the United States in specific.

∼ WESTERN DRESS CODE, PRIMARILY FOR WOMEN: Arabs cite the totally unacceptable Western dress which reveals a woman's anatomy by allowing tight, formfitting, low-cut, breast-revealing blouses and dresses and short shorts which reveal the shape and contours of the most private areas of the female anatomy. To Arabs, this is a sign of socially condoned promiscuity and a value void (Chapter 8, "Honor").

∼ WESTERN PUBLIC DISPLAY OF AFFECTION: In the Arab world, male-female intimacy is reserved for private expression only. Western public kissing, hugging, touching, and caressing, even at airport send-offs, if prolonged, is at the very least in bad taste and unacceptable public behavior (Chapter 8, "Honor").

∼ WESTERN ACCEPTANCE OF OPEN HOMOSEXUALITY: Open expression of homosexuality is even less acceptable in the Arab and Muslim world than is the public display and expression of heterosexual affection. It is considered repulsive, deviant, unnatural, vile, and the ultimate perversion of God's plan (Chapter 8, "Honor"). As with adultery, homosexuality is punishable by death in Islam.

∼ WESTERN PRODUCTION AND TOLERANCE OF PORNOGRAPHY: To the Arab world, it clearly demonstrates moral decay and corruption of values. It is also considered to be a total exploitation of and dishonor to women (Chapter 8, "Honor").

⮑ CHILD ABUSE IN ALL ITS PERVERTED FORMS: In the Arab mind, child abuse is inexcusable and should be dealt with in the harshest manner possible; execution if it involves the death of a child. Arabs view children as a gift from God. Children are given to people in trust to nurture, care for, and to teach of God's love and goodness. A violation of this trust produces rage in the eyes and hearts of Arabs.

At its core, the Middle East-West conflict is a cultural and ideological clash. From the Middle East comes a strict, narrow, seventh century extremist puritanical interpretation of Islamic values with the narrowest reading of the *Qur'an* as its guide. From the West comes a most liberal secular separation of church and state position, championed by individual freedoms of expression and action devoid of religious or governmental control. The Middle East sees all the ills of the West and attributes them to moral decay resulting from a bankrupt value system. Puritanical and extremist Islam and the supporters of traditional strict Arab values are fearful that if they embrace the West and its culture, the West's immorality and amorality will invade Middle Eastern culture and destroy it from within, as they perceive it to be destroying the West. For this reason, some voices at the fringes of Muslim and Arab culture have developed an extremist position for not wanting Arab lands and their people to be "contaminated" by Western moral decay and consider it a divine calling to oppose the infiltration of Western culture into their society.

In reality, neither the West nor the Middle East is dominated by extremist thinking. Both the Bin Ladins of the world, with their vile view of the West, and those in the West who think all Arabs and Muslims are murdering terrorists are wrong in their generalizations. Both cultures are dominated by rational, tolerant people who value life and who welcome the richness of religious and cultural diversity. Both societies need to rid themselves of extremist thinking, which can never be constructive, but can only destroy and cause greater mistrust, hatred, and animosity. The Middle East and the West should continue to celebrate each other's cultural heritage, richness, and diversity, taking that which is good and positive from the other.

As a final word of caution and encouragement, the Middle East and the West should guard against being quick to draw negative judgments of the other and categorically reject each other's culture. Both cultures can and should observe, learn, and draw from the richness and goodness of each other's cultural heritage. While the Middle East can learn and benefit much from Western technology, scientific and medical advancement, and respect for the value of the individual, the West can learn much from Arab values, morality, and norms of decency and respect, and the importance of preserving the life of the community.

# Appendix A

# Useful Expressions

**B**elow are some useful expressions which are important to anyone traveling through the Middle East. Arabs do not generally expect non-Arabs, especially Westerners, to be able to speak any Arabic and are extremely pleased when foreigners make an attempt to do so. I recommend that you use your Arabic language skills, no matter how limited, whenever possible, as this will demonstrate a deeper level of interest by you (the foreigner) in your Arab host and his culture. The following words and phrases are written in a commonly used conversational form and not in the Classical or Modern Standard Arabic, which is how Arabic is normally written. However, these phrases will be understood across the Arab world and will bring smiles to the Arabs with whom you are attempting to communicate.

In order for you to more accurately read the following words and phrases, a few pronunciation guides are provided below. One of the most striking differences between English and Arabic is that Arabic has some guttural sounds formed in the back of the throat, which may be difficult for English speakers to replicate.

1. The capital "H" (a sound I describe to my students as being much like Darth Vader's breathing, which I call the "Vader H") is formed in the back of the throat by constricting

the muscles of the throat and aspirating. This sound is similar to the sound you would make when cleaning the lenses of your eyeglasses.

2. The "kh" combination is a single sound in Arabic and is also formed in the back of the throat. This sound is similar to the sound you would make when trying to clear something from the back of your throat. For those readers who are familiar with the German or Dutch languages, this "kh" sound is similar to the guttural sounds of those languages.

3. Similar to the "kh" above, the "gh" combination is also a single sound in Arabic. The sound of this letter combination is identical to the French "r." For those unfamiliar with the sound of the French "r," it is made by gargling a small amount of saliva in the back of the throat as the sound is being made.

4. The Arabic "r" is pronounced exactly the same way as the Spanish "r." In other words, the Arabic "r" is always rolled or trilled.

5. Double vowels, such as "aa" and "ee," are to be elongated or stretched out, as in the words "ash" and "eel," respectively. Similarly, the double "oo" is also elongated, such as in the words "tool" and "boot."

6. Single vowels, a, e, i, o and u, are pronounced as short vowels, as in the words "ask," "edge," "it," "obtain," and "up."

7. An (m) or (f) following an Arabic word or phrase indicates that it is gender specific and should be used when addressing a male or female, respectively. The Arabic is followed by an English translation also using the (m) and (f) designation, indicating gender. Arabic always uses gender distinction when addressing someone, and as in Spanish, all nouns are

either male or female. Words and phrases with the same meaning but the opposite gender are given the same chronological number in the list of useful expressions.

8. The apostrophe (') is used to signify a guttural Arabic sound not found in English. It is formed by constricting the muscles in the back of the throat and making an "a" or an "i" sound (depending on what vowel follows), not too unlike the sound you would make if you were being choked. You can try to make this sound by simulating choking yourself by **gently** applying pressure with your thumbs against the front of your throat and your fingers behind your neck, and then attempting to make the "a" sound. Or you could just ignore trying to make the sound altogether and simply hesitate where the (') belongs and add a short "a" or "i" (depending on what vowel follows) instead of attempting all these heroics. This sound is probably the hardest sound for Westerners to make. Now get started and don't worry about sounding funny; you are actually speaking Arabic!

### BASIC CONVERSATIONAL EXPRESSIONS

| ENGLISH PHRASE | ARABIC TRANSLATION |
|---|---|
| 1. Hi/hello | *marHaba* |
| 2. Hi/hello, response | *marHabtein* |
| 3. Good-bye and good-bye response | *ma' issalaama* |
| 4. Normally a Muslim greeting "peace be to you" (pl) | *assalaamu 'aleikum* |
| 5. Muslim greeting response "and to you peace" (pl) | *wa'aleikum assalaam* |
| 6. Good morning | *sabaH alkhair* |
| 7. Good morning response | *sabaH annoor* |
| 8. Good afternoon/evening | *masaa alkhair* |

9. Good afternoon/evening response — *masaa annoor*

10. How are you? (m), polite — *keef Haalak? (m)*
    How are you? (f), polite — *keef Haalik? (f)*

11. How are you? (pl) — *keef Haalkum? (pl)*

12. How are you? (m), casual — *keefak? (m)*
    How are you? (f), casual — *keefik? (f)*

13. How are you? (pl), casual — *keefkum? (pl)*

14. I/me — *ana*

15. Fine (m) — *qwayyis (m)*
    Fine (f) — *qwayyisah (f)*

16. I am fine (m) — *ana qwayyis (m)*
    I am fine (f) — *ana quayyisah (f)*

17. God willing (in response to EVERYTHING!) — *Inshallah*

18. I am tired (m) — *ana ta'baan (m)*
    I am tired (f) — *ana ta'baanah (f)*

19. I am sleepy (m) — *ana na'saan (m)*
    I am sleepy (f) — *ana na'saanah (f)*

20. Please (m) — *min fadlak (m)*
    Please (f) — *min fadlik (f)*

21. If you please (m) — *tafaddal (m)*
    If you please (f) — *tafaddali (f)*

22. Thank you — *shukran*

23. You are welcome — *'afwan*

24. Praise be to God (in response to "how are you") — *al-Hamdu lillaah*

25. We thank God (in response to "how are you") — *nushkur Allah*

26. Where is the bathroom, please? (m) — *wein ilHammaam min fadlak? (m)*
    Where is the bathroom, please? (f) — *wein ilHammaam min fadlik? (f)*

27. Where is the police, please? (m) — *wein ish-shurtah min fadlak? (m)*

|  | Where is the police, please? (f) | *wein ish-shurtah min fadlik? (f)* |
|---|---|---|
| 28. | Where is the American embassy? | *wein issafaarah lam rikiyyah?* |
| 29. | Can you help me, please? (m) | *mumkin tisaa'idni min fadlak? (m)* |
|  | Can you help me, please? (f) | *mumkin tisaa'ideeni min fadlik? (f)* |
| 30. | Can you (m) take me to the American Embassy? | *mumkin takhudni lis safaarah alamrikiyyah? (m)* |
|  | Can you (f) take me to the American Embassy? | *mumkin takhudeeni lissafaarah alamrikiyyah? (f)* |
| 31. | Teacher/professor (m) | *ustaath (m)* |
|  | Teacher/professor (f) | *ustaathah (f)* |
| 32. | Question | *suaal* |
| 33. | Question, please (m) | *suaal min fadlak (m)* |
|  | Question, please (f) | *suaal min fadlik (f)* |
| 34. | I have a question | *fee 'indi suaal* |
| 35. | Yes (casual, "yeah") | *aiwa* |
| 36. | Yes (polite) | *na'am* |
| 37. | No | *la'* |
| 38. | I speak | *batkallam* |
| 39. | Arabic | *'arabi* |
| 40. | I am learning Arabic in a university | *ana bat'allam 'arabi fi jaami'ah* |
| 41. | I speak Arabic | *ana batkallam 'arabi* |
| 42. | A little | *shwai* |
| 43. | I speak a little Arabic | *ana batkallam 'arabi shwai* |
| 44. | I don't speak Arabic | *ana maa batkallam 'arabi* |

| | | |
|---|---|---|
| 45. | I am learning Arabic | *ana bat'allam 'arabi* |
| 46. | How much is the price? | *kam assi'ir?* |
| 47. | This | *Haatha* |
| 48. | How much is this? | *kam si'ir haatha?* |
| 49. | I am thirsty (m)<br>I am thirsty (f) | *ana 'atshaan (m)*<br>*ana 'atshaanah (f)* |
| 50. | I am hungry (m)<br>I am hungry (f) | *ana ju'aan (m)*<br>*ana ju'aanah (f)* |
| 51. | What | *aeish* |
| 52. | Is/are there, or there is/are | *fee* |
| 53. | Food | *akill* |
| 54. | I want to eat | *ana biddi aakul* |
| 55. | I want to drink | *ana biddi ashrab* |
| 56. | You (m)<br>You (f) | *inta (m)*<br>*inti (f)* |
| 57. | What is your (m) name?<br>What is your (f) name? | *aeish ismak*<br>*aeish ismik* |
| 58. | My Name is | *ismi* |

## RESTAURANT VOCABULARY

| | | |
|---|---|---|
| 1. | What is there to eat? | *aeish fee lilakil?* |
| 2. | Is there grilled (skewered) meat? | *fee laHim mashwi?* |
| 3. | Is there kabob? | *fee kabaab?* |
| 4. | Is there kaftah?<br>(skewered ground meat with spices) | *fee kaftah?* |
| 5. | Is there grilled beef? | *fee laHim baqar mashwi?* |
| 6. | Is there grilled lamb? | *fee laHim kharoof mashwi* |
| 7. | Is there grilled chicken? | *fee dajaaj mashwi?* |
| 8. | Is there rice? | *fee ruzz?* |

| | |
|---|---|
| 9. Is there salad? | *fee salatah?* |
| 10. Are there fried potatoes? | *fee batata maslooq?* |
| 11. Are there French fries? | *fee cheeps?* |
| 12. Are there fried eggs? | *fee beid maslooq?* |
| 13. Are there boiled eggs? | *fee beid maqli?* |
| 14. Is there cheese? | *fee jibni?* |
| 15. Is there yogurt? | *fee laban?* |
| 16. Is there fruit? | *fee faakiha?* |
| 17. Are there apples? | *fee tuffaaH?* |
| 18. Are there bananas? | *fee moze?* |
| 19. Are there oranges? | *fee burtuqaal?* |
| 20. Are there vegetables? | *fee khudaar?* |
| 21. Are there potatoes? | *fee bataatah?* |
| 22. Are there tomatoes? | *fee bandorah?* |
| 23. Is there lettuce? | *fee khass?* |
| 24. Are there onions? | *fee basal?* |
| 25. Is there squash/zucchini? | *fee koosa?* |
| 26. Is there something sweet? (dessert) | *fee shi Hilu?* |
| 27. What is there sweet? (dessert) | *aeish fee Hilu?* |
| 28. Is there Baklava? | *fee baqlawa?* |
| 29. What is there to drink? | *aeish fee lish-shurb?* |
| 30. Is there water? | *fee mai?* |
| 31. Is there Cola? | *fee cola?* |
| 32. Is there orange juice? | *fee 'aseer burtuqaal?* |
| 33. Is there apple juice? | *fee 'aseer tuffaaH?* |
| 34. Is there beer? | *fee beerah?* |

35. Is there tea? (only hot tea is served)     *fee shai?*

36. Is there coffee?     *fee qahwa?*

37. Is there American coffee?     *fee qahwa amrikiyyah?*

38. Is there Nescafe?
(euphemism for American coffee)     *fee nescafe?*

39. May I have water (coffee, tea)?     *mumkin mai (qahwa, shai)?*

40. May I have the bill please (m)?     *mumkin al-fatoorah min fadlak? (m)*

      May I have the bill please (f)?     *mumkin al-fatoorah min fadlik? (f)*

## Days Of The Week

The word for day in Arabic is yom and serves the same purpose as the suffix "day" does in English when referring to the days of the week. Although the word yom should be stated before saying the actual day of the week, most Arabs leave it out in casual, familiar conversation and simply say *al-aHad, al-ithnein, ath-thalaatha,* etc. However, Classical and Modern Standard Arabic retains the usage of the word yom in speaking formally and in writing. The Arabic spelling of the days of the week below is intended as a pronunciation guide and does not reflect the accurate Arabic written form of the word, which in some cases is different.

1. Sunday     *yom al-aHad*

2. Monday     *yom al-ithnein*

3. Tuesday     *yom ath-thalaatha*

4. Wednesday     *yom al-arba'a*

5. Thursday     *yom al-khamees*

6. Friday     *yom al-jum'a*

7. Saturday     *yom as-sabt*

## MONTHS OF THE YEAR

| English | Arabized Western | Arabic |
|---------|-----------------|--------|
| 1. January | *yanayir* | *kanoon ath-thaani* |
| 2. February | *fabrayir* | *shbaat* |
| 3. March | *maris* | *aathaar* |
| 4. April | *abril* | *nisaan* |
| 5. May | *maayu* | *aiyaar* |
| 6. June | *yoonyu* | *Huzaiyraan* |
| 7. July | *yoolyu* | *tammooz* |
| 8. August | *oghustus* | *aab* |
| 9. September | *sebtembar* | *aiylool* |
| 10. October | *oktobar* | *tishreen al-awwal* |
| 11. November | *nofembar* | *tishreen ath-thaani* |
| 12. December | *decembar* | *kanoon al-awwal* |

# Appendix B

# The Arabic Sound and Script

rabic is a Semitic language which is written from right to left. There are no capital letters in Arabic, and Arabic is always written in a cursive script, never in block letters as is an option in English. There are twenty-eight letters in the Arabic alphabet. Each letter is written four different ways depending on where it appears in a word. If the letter is the first letter in a word it is written in the **initial position**. If the letter is not the first letter in a word and not the last letter in a word it is written in the **medial position**. If the letter is written as the last letter in a word it is written in the **final position**. And if the letter is not connected to any other letter it is written in the **independent position** (see rule below under "Special Letter Formation," number 4). In addition to the twenty-eight regular letters, which include the long a, i, and o vowels, Arabic has three short a, i, and o vowels, as well as eight other diacritical markers which are written above and below the letters (see section below on "Short Vowels and Diacritical Markers").

When reading the Arabic alphabet and pronouncing the Arabic letters below, letters that are underlined (such as the kh and the gh in Appendix A) should be read as one sound similar to the way the "t" and the "h" and the "s" and the "h" are combined in English to produce the "th" and "sh" sounds, respectively. These letters are never to be pronounced as separate "kh" and "gh" sounds.

Arabic has some duplicative sounding letters to the Western ear. This is because some letters in Arabic are formed at the front of the mouth, called "dental letters," and others are formed in the back of the mouth and/or throat and are called "guttural letters." The guttural letters are identified below in **bold letters**. There is no consistency in how Arabic vowels are pronounced, but as a general rule they do not have an American diphthong, or "twang," but more of a European/Spanish short pronunciation.

Below, the names of the Arabic letters, an approximation of their English pronunciation, the sound of the letters, and the Arabic letters in the independent positions are presented. The Arabic short vowels and diacritical markers are not written out in Arabic, but only presented and identified for their role and position in the Arabic Sound and Script System.

## THE ARABIC ALPHABET

| ARABIC NAME | ENGLISH APPROXIMATION | SOUND | ARABIC LETTER |
|---|---|---|---|
| 1. *alif* | aa | a | ١ |
| 2. *baa* | b | b | ب |
| 3. *taa* | t | t | ت |
| 4. *thaa* | th | th (thin) | ث |
| 5. *jeem* | j | j | ج |
| 6. **Haa** | **H** (no English equivalent) | H (throaty) | ح |
| 7. **khaa** | **kh** | **kh** (guttural) | خ |
| 8. *daal* | d | d | د |
| 9. *thaal* | th | th (this) | ذ |
| 10. *raa* | r | r (Spanish 'r') | ر |
| 11. *zaa* | z | z | ز |

| ARABIC NAME | ENGLISH APPROXIMATION | SOUND | ARABIC LETTER |
|---|---|---|---|
| 12. *seen* | s | s | س |
| 13. *sheen* | sh | sh | ش |
| 14. **sod** | **s** | **s** | ص |
| 15. **dod** | **d** | **d** | ض |
| 16. **taa** | **t** | **t** | ط |
| 17. **thaa** | **th** | **th** (the) | ظ |
| 18. **ein** | **ei** (no English equivalent) | **ei** (guttural) | ع |
| 19. **ghein** | **ghe** (no English equivalent) | **gh** (French 'r') | غ |
| 20. *faa* | f | f | ف |
| 21. **qaaf** | **q** | **q** | ق |
| 22. *kaaf* | k | k | ك |
| 23. *laam* | l | l | ل |
| 24. *meem* | m | m | م |
| 25. *noon* | n | n | ن |
| 26. *haa* | h | h (aspirated) | ه |
| 27. *waoo* | w, oo | w, oo | و |
| 28. *yaa* | e, i, y | ee, i, y | ي |

❋

## SPECIAL LETTER FORMATIONS

1. The combination of the *laam* in the initial or medial positions followed by the *alif* is called a *laam-alif* construct and is written as one unit.

2. The *taa marbootah* is formed by adding two superscript dots above the final and independent position *haa*. A *taa marbootah* is pronounced as a *taa*.

3. The *alif maksoorah* is formed by deleting the two subscript dots below the *yaa*. The *alif maksoorah* is pronounced as an *alif*.

4. The following letters are <u>never</u> connected to another letter in the forward position; i.e., no letter may be connected to them after they are formed but the previous letter written may be connected to them before they are formed:

*alif* (a)          *daal* (d)          *waoo* (w, oo)

*raa* (r)           *thaal* (th)        *zaa* (z)

## SHORT VOWELS AND DIACRITICAL MARKERS

1. *FatHah* ´ : Short 'a' written above a letter.

2. *FatHataan* ˶ : (Meaning two *fatHahs*). Pronounced 'ann' and written above a letter.

3. *Kasrah* ˏ : Short 'i' written below a letter.

4. *Kasrataan* ˳ : (Meaning two *kasrahs*). Pronounced 'inn' and written below a letter.

5. *Dammah* ˏ : Short 'o' written above a letter.

6. *Dummahtaan* ˮ : (Meaning two *dammahs*). Pronounced 'unn' and written above a letter.

7. *Sukoon* ° : Indicates silence, or no vowel sound added, written above a letter.

8. *Hamza* ء : Glottal stop (an abrupt stop to the flow of air through the throat as a letter is being formed), written above or below an *alif*, on a letter "seat," or free-standing.

9. *Shaddah* ّ : Always written above a letter, which results in the letter below it being emphasized/accented (Arabs refer to it as doubling the letter).

10. *Dagger alif* ١ : Pronounced as an *alif* and written above a letter.

11. *Maddah* ~ : Pronounced as an elongated *alif*, usually written above an initial *alif*

# Appendix C

# Arabic Numbers

rab traders first came in contact with numbers when they traveled to India. The nature of their business, trade, necessitated a sound knowledge and use of numbers and mathematics. Arab traders and mathematicians took the Indian numbering system and added to it the zero, thereby inventing the decimal system as we know it today. The addition of the zero opened up a world of possibilities, now that man's brain could think and function in the realm of both positive and negative numbers. This made such fields as algebra, alchemy, astronomy, navigation, and advanced mathematics possible. Many scientific and mathematical words we use in English, which start with al (the Arabic definite article), are in fact, Arabic words.

Below I have written out Arabic numbers phonetically with their English translations which will help the reader to engage in minor mathematical activities such as asking the price of an item and telling time. Although the Arabic script is written from right to left (see Appendix B), Arabic numbers are written and read in the same order as is English. The numbers resulting from adding one to the tens (21, 22, 33, 34, 45, 46, etc.) are produced by saying the one integer desired first (1, 2, 3, 4, etc.), followed by the ten integer desired (20, 30, 40, etc.); i.e., one and twenty, two and twenty, one and thirty, two and thirty, one and forty, two and forty, etc.

## ONE TO TEN

| One | *waHad* | Six | *sittah* |
|-----|---------|-----|----------|
| Two | *ithnein* | Seven | *sab'ah* |
| Three | *thalaatha* | Eight | *thamanyah* |
| Four | *arba'a* | Nine | *tis'ah* |
| Five | *khamsa* | Ten | *'asharah* |

## ELEVEN TO TWENTY

| Eleven | *iHda'ish* | Sixteen | *sitta'ish* |
|--------|-----------|---------|-------------|
| Twelve | *itna'ish* | Seventeen | *saba'ta'ish* |
| Thirteen | *thalata'ish* | Eighteen | *thamanta'ish* |
| Fourteen | *arba'ta'ish* | Nineteen | *tisi'ta'ish* |
| Fifteen | *khamista'ish* | Twenty | *'ishreen* |

## "TEENS" PRONUNCIATION GUIDE

In construct with another word, add an "ar" sound to the end of numbers 11–19 for correct pronunciation; i.e., when counting objects such as thirteen children, twelve eggs, etc.

| Eleven | *iHda'shar* |
|--------|-------------|
| Twelve | *itna'shar* |
| Thirteen | *thalata'shar* |
| Fourteen | *arba'ta'shar* |
| Fifteen | *khamista'shar* |
| Sixteen | *sitta'shar* |
| Seventeen | *saba'ta'shar* |
| Eighteen | *thamanta'shar* |
| Nineteen | *tisi'ta'shar* |

### TWENTY-ONE TO THIRTY

| | |
|---|---|
| Twenty-one | *waHad wa'ishreen* |
| Twenty-two | *ithnein wa'ishreen* |
| Twenty-three | *thalaatha wa'ishreen* |
| Twenty-four | *arba'a wa'ishreen* |
| Twenty-five | *khamsa wa'ishreen* |
| Twenty-six | *sitta wa'ishreen* |
| Twenty-seven | *sab'a wa'ishreen* |
| Twenty-eight | *thamanya wa'shreen* |
| Twenty-nine | *tis'a wa'ishreen* |
| Thirty | *thalatheen* |

### THIRTY-ONE TO FORTY

| | |
|---|---|
| Thirty-one | *waHad wathalatheen* |
| Thirty-two | *ithnein wathalatheen* |
| Thirty-three | *thalaatha wathalatheen* |
| Thirty-four | *araba'a wathalatheen* |
| Thirty-five | *khamsa wathalatheen* |
| Thirty-six | *sitta wathalatheen* |
| Thirty-seven | *sab'a wathalatheen* |
| Thirty-eight | *thamanya wathalatheen* |
| Thirty-nine | *tis'a wathalatheen* |
| Forty | *arba'een* |

### FORTY-ONE TO FIFTY

| | |
|---|---|
| Forty-one | *waHad waarba'een* |
| Forty-two | *ithnein waarba'een* |
| Forty-three | *thalaatha waarba'een* |
| Forty-four | *arba'a waarba'een* |
| Forty-five | *khamsa waarba'een* |
| Forty-six | *sitta waarba'een* |
| Forty-seven | *sab'a waarba'een* |
| Forty-eight | *thamanya waarba'een* |
| Forty-nine | *tis'a waarba'een* |
| Fifty | *khamseen* |

## TENS

| Ten | 'ashara |
|---|---|
| Twenty | 'ishreen |
| Thirty | thalatheen |
| Forty | arba'een |
| Fifty | khamseen |
| Sixty | sitteen |
| Seventy | sab'een |
| Eighty | thamaneen |
| Ninety | tis'een |

## HUNDREDS

| One hundred | miyyah |
|---|---|
| Two hundred | miyyatein |
| Three hundred | thalat miyyah |
| Four hundred | arba' miyyah |
| Five hundred | khamis miyyah |
| Six hundred | sitt miyyah |
| Seven hundred | sabi' miyyah |
| Eight hundred | thaman miyyah |
| Nine hundred | tisi' miyyah |

## THOUSANDS

| One thousand | alf |
|---|---|
| Two thousand | alfein |
| Three thousand | thalat alaaf |
| Four thousand | arba' alaaf |
| Five thousand | khamis alaaf |
| Six thousand | sit alaaf |
| Seven thousand | sabi' alaaf |
| Eight thousand | thaman alaaf |
| Nine thousand | tisi' alaaf |

# Appendix D

# The Ninety-Nine Names of Allah (God)

| TRANSLATED/MEANING | ARABIC PRONUNCIATion |
|---|---|
| 1. The Singular | *al-WaHeed* |
| 2. The Alone | *al-AHad* |
| 3. The Eternal | *al-Samad* |
| 4. The Mighty | *al-Qaadir* |
| 5. The Powerful | *al-Muqtadir* |
| 6. The First | *al-Awwal* |
| 7. The Last | *al-Aakhir* |
| 8. The Manifest | *al-thaahir* |
| 9. The Hidden | *al-Baatin* |
| 10. The Governor | *al-Waali* |
| 11. The Exalted | *al-Muta'aali* |
| 12. The Pious | *al-Barr* |
| 13. The Forgiving | *al-Tawwaab* |
| 14. The Pardoner | *al-'Afoow* |
| 15. The Compassionate | *al-Ra'oof* |
| 16. The Gatherer | *al-Jaami'* |
| 17. The Self-Sufficient | *al-Ghaniyy* |
| 18. The Light | *al-Noor* |
| 19. The Guide | *al-Haadi* |
| 20. The Innovator | *al-Badee'* |
| 21. The Lord | *al-Rabb* |
| 22. The Manifest | *al-Mubayyin* |
| 23. The Mighty | *al-Qadeer* |

| TRANSLATED/MEANING | ARABIC PRONUNCIATION |
|---|---|
| 24. The Protector | *al-Haafith* |
| 25. The Surety | *al-Kafeel* |
| 26. The Appreciative | *al-Shaakir* |
| 27. The Most Bounteous | *al-Akram* |
| 28. The Creative | *al-Khallaaq* |
| 29. The Patron | *al-Mawlla* |
| 30. The Helper | *al-Naseer* |
| 31. The God | *al-Ilaah* |
| 32. God | *Allah* |
| 33. The Merciful | *al-Rahmaan* |
| 34. The Clement | *al-RaHeem* |
| 35. The Ruler | *al-Malik* |
| 36. The Pure | *al-Quddoos* |
| 37. The Safe | *al-Salaam* |
| 38. The Secure | *al-Mu'min* |
| 39. The Controller | *al-Muhaymin* |
| 40. The Honorable | *al-'Azeez* |
| 41. The Compeller | *al-Jabbaar* |
| 42. The Proud | *al-Mutakabbir* |
| 43. The Creator | *al-Khaaliq* |
| 44. The Maker | *al-Baari'* |
| 45. The Fashioner | *al-Musawwir* |
| 46. The Forgiver | *al-Ghaffaar* |
| 47. The Dominant | *al-Qahhaar* |
| 48. The Bestower | *al-Wahhaab* |
| 49. The Provider | *al-Razzaaq* |
| 50. The Opener | *al-FattaaH* |
| 51. The Knower | *al-'Aleem* |
| 52. The Hearer | *al-Sammee'* |
| 53. The Seer | *al-Baseer* |
| 54. The Kind | *al-Lateef* |
| 55. The Expert | *al-Khabeer* |
| 56. The Forebearing | *al-Haleem* |
| 57. The Magnificent | *al-'Atheem* |
| 58. The Forgiving | *al-Ghafoor* |
| 59. The Thankful | *al-Shakoor* |

| TRANSLATED/MEANING | ARABIC PRONUNCIATION |
|---|---|
| 60. The Lofty | al-'Aliyy |
| 61. The Great | al-Kabeer |
| 62. The Preserver | al-Hafeeth |
| 63. The Omniscient | al-'Allaam |
| 64. The Omnipotent | al-Qaahir |
| 65. The Forgiver | al-Ghaafir |
| 66. The Creator | al-Faatir |
| 67. The Sovereign | al-Maleek |
| 68. The Gracious | al-Hafiyy |
| 69. The All-Pervading | al-MuHeet |
| 70. The Called for Help | al-Musta'aan |
| 71. The Sublime | al-Rafee' |
| 72. The Sufficient One | al-Kaafee |
| 73. Predominant | Ghaalib |
| 74. The Gracious | al-Mannaan |
| 75. The Glorious | al-Jaleel |
| 76. The Giver of Life | al-MuHayyee |
| 77. The Giver of Death | al-Mumeet |
| 78. The Inheritor | al-Waarith |
| 79. The Awakener | al-Baa'ith |
| 80. The Everlasting One | al-Baaqi |
| 81. The Truth | al-Haqq |
| 82. The Trustee | al-Wakeel |
| 83. The Strong | al-Qawiyy |
| 84. The Firm | al-Mateen |
| 85. The Guardian | al-Waliyy |
| 86. The Praiseworthy | al-Hameed |
| 87. The Alive | al-Haiyy |
| 88. The Self-Sustaining | al-Qayyoom |
| 89. The Amicable | al-Wadood |
| 90. The Glorious | al-Majeed |
| 91. The Witness | al-Shaheed |
| 92. The Wise | al-Hakeem |
| 93. The Nourisher | al-Muqeet |
| 94. The Reckoner | al-Haseeb |
| 95. The Generous One | al-Kareem |

| TRANSLATED/MEANING | ARABIC PRONUNCIATION |
|---|---|
| 96. The Watchful | *al-Raqeeb* |
| 97. The Near | *al-Qareeb* |
| 98. The Responsive | *al-Mujeeb* |
| 99. The Vast | *al-Waasi'* |

# Glossary

***Abayah.*** A loose outer robe, usually black and covering the entire body, worn in public by Arab Muslim women over their clothing worn at home.

***Abu.*** Arabic for "father" or in coustruct "father of." In the Arabic culture, men take on a social name by being called "father of" their oldest male child, such as "*Abu Omar*" for the father of *Omar,* and if they only have daughters, "father of" their oldest daughter.

***al.*** The Arabic definite article "the." In Arabic, the definite article is a prefix to a word and rarely stands alone as a separate word. Many scientific and especially many mathematical words used in English having the prefix "al" have their origin in Arabic, such as algebra, alchemy, alcohol, almanac.

***Allah.*** Arabic for God. In pre-Islamic Arabia, *Allah* was the supreme deity in the Arabian Peninsula's polytheistic religion.

***"Allahu Akbar."*** The Islamic declaration professing that God is omnipotent or supreme. Sometimes translated into English as "God is Great."

***al-Qaida.*** A terrorist organization established by Usama Bin Ladin.

***al-Ummah al-Arabiyyah.*** The concept that all Arabs are linked or related to the "Greater Arab Nation" or family of nations. This concept encompasses all Arab nations across national boundaries in a confederation of one people linked by their common cultural, linguistic, and religious heritage.

*al-Watan al-Arabi.* See *al-Ummah al-Arabiyyah.*

**Anwar Sadat.** President of Egypt from 1969 to 1981. President Sadat was assassinated by Muslim extremists while reviewing a parade in Cairo commemorating the 1973 Ramadan (Yom Kippur) War.

**Arab League.** See League of Arab States.

**Arabic.** The language of the Arabs. A Semitic people who originated in the Arabian Peninsula who speak the Arabic language. Other Semitic languages include Hebrew and Aramaic.

**Arabized.** The conquest of a people or culture by Arab Muslim armies in the seventh and eighth centuries A.D. People such as modern-day Lebanese whose ancestors were originally Phoenicians and later became a mix of many conquerors who over the centuries of Arab Muslim rule lost their original cultural identity and gradually became "Cultural Arabs" (see definition below) or Arabized.

**Arabs.** Descendants of Semitic tribes from the Arabian Peninsula. Today, as defined by the Arab League of Nations, anyone who has lived in the Middle East, speaks Arabic, and identifies with the Arab culture.

**Balfour Declaration.** The 1917 declaration by the British government through its foreign secretary, Lord Balfour, to establish a Jewish homeland in Palestine.

**Bedu (Bedouin).** The Arab nomadic tribes who roam the Middle East in search of water and grazing lands for their herds of sheep, goats, and camels.

**Bekka' Valley.** The region in Lebanon east of the Shuff Mountains and west of the Syrian border.

**Consensus.** The traditional Arab decision-making method employed by clan and tribal leaders (*sheikhs,* emirs, and kings), which is continued in modern times by Arab heads of state. Consensus decision-making is paramount in the Arab world, particularly when decisions have regional impact, such as decisions involving Israel. An example of an Arab leader breaking with Arab consensus decision-making occurred in 1977 when President Anwar Sadat traveled to Israel, a move that ultimately cost President Sadat his life.

**Cultural Arabs.** Anyone who has lived in the Arab world, speaks the Arabic language, and identifies with the Arab culture. Cultural Arabs may or may not be racially or ethnically Arab.

**Defense Attaché Office (DAO).** The office within embassies responsible for military-to-military relations between two countries.

**Deputy Chief of Mission (DCM).** The second in command to the ambassador in an embassy. The DCM assumes the title of Chargé d'Affaires in the ambassador's absence.

**Diaspora.** The dispersion of the Jewish people from their ancestral homeland in Palestine beginning in 70 A.D. when the Romans destroyed Jewish rule in Judea and Samaria.

**Ehud Barak.** A former Chief of the General Staff of the Israeli Defense Forces who became the Labor Party Prime Minister of Israel in the late 1990s and who succeeded Benjamin Netanyahu and preceded Ariel Sharon as Prime Minister.

*Fatwa.* An Islamic religious decree declared by a qualified cleric. Most recently, the West has become familiar with this word because Bin Ladin (who is not a qualified Muslim cleric) has illegitimately issued a *Fatwa,* calling for Muslims to kill "crusaders and Zionists" (a euphemism for Westerners, particularly Americans and Israelis).

**Five Pillars of Islam.** Five imperatives required of all Muslims: profession of faith ("there is no God but *Allah* and Muhammad is his messenger"), prayer (five times a day), almsgiving, fasting (during the holy month of Ramadan), and a pilgrimage to the holy city of Makkah (at least once in a lifetime if one is financially and physically able).

*Ghutra.* An Arabian Peninsular man's head covering, consisting of either a white, black and white checked, or red and white checked scarf-like head covering, secured by a black rope-like cord. Known in the Levant as a *hattah* and an '*igaal.*

**Guilt Based Culture.** A culture which controls conformity to its values and norms through guilt.

*Haj/Hajah.* Arabic for pilgrimage or pilgrim. Often given as a social title to someone who has completed a pilgrimage to the holy city of Makkah as prescribed by one of the Five Pillars of Islam.

*Hareem.* In its most correct form, Arabic for "women." Often referred to in the West as "harem" with the connotation of multiple wives and concubines of a wealthy Arab *sheikh.*

**Husni Mubarak.** President of Egypt since Anwar Sadat's assassination in 1981.

**Immam.** Muslim religious scholars who lead Muslim worship and deliver the Friday sermons in mosques. Although Islam claims not to have a clergy, Immams serve in that capacity.

*Inshallah.* The Arab response to virtually everything, meaning "God willing." This phrase usually means yes when spoken in response to a question.

**Islam.** The religion of the followers of the teachings of the Prophet Muhammad. Islam, in Arabic, means submission, submission to the will of *Allah*/God.

*Hijrah.* Arabic for migration. Significant to Islam because it refers to the year 622 A.D. when the Prophet Muhammad fled (migrated) from the city of Makkah to the city of Yathrib (Madina).

**Jebusites.** The inhabitants of the region in and around Jerusalem (known as Jebus) prior to King David's making Jerusalem the Jewish capital around 900 B.C.

*Jihad.* To struggle, toil, strive, exert, put forth effort and diligence. Now interpreted in the West as meaning "Holy War."

*Ka'bah.* The large cube-shaped structure in the city of Makkah in Saudi Arabia which is the object of Islamic worship and which predates Islam as a place of worship. The cube contains a black stone, probably a meteorite, believed by Muslims to have been placed there by Abraham.

**Khadijah.** Muhammad's wealthy first wife, a widow whom he married when he was twenty-five and she was forty years old.

*Kafir.* Arabic-Muslim word for a nonbeliever (non-Muslim). Also means heathen, infidel, and enemy of God.

**League of Arab States,** often simply, **Arab League.** A confederation of Arab cultural countries consisting of the following twenty-two states: Algeria, Bahrain, Comoros, Djibouti, Egypt, Iraq, Jordan, Kuwait, Lebanon, Libya, Mauritania, Morocco, Oman, Palestine (a member of the Arab League, although not yet recognized as a sovereign nation), Qatar, Saudi Arabia, Somalia, Sudan, Syria, Tunisia, the United Arab Emirates (UAE), and Yemen.

**Makkah.** The coastal city on the western edge of the Arabian Peninsula, which is the birthplace of both the Prophet Muhammad and the Muslim religion, Islam.

*Manat, Uzza, Allat.* The three most important gods in pre-Islamic Arabia, ruled by the higher deity known as *Allah.*

**McMahon-Sharif Hussein Correspondence.** A series of correspondence in 1915 from the Sharif (Governor) Hussein of the Hijaaz (the west coastal region of the Arabian Peninsula, which includes Makkah), to General McMahon, the commander of the British forces in the Middle East stationed in Cairo, requesting autonomy for the Arabs in former Ottoman Empire lands once the Ottoman Turks were defeated.

**MIG.** A type of Russian-built fighter aircraft, named for its two Russian designers, Mikoyan and Gurevich.

**Middle East.** The geographical area bounded by Egypt on the west, Iran on the east, Turkey to the north, and Yemen to the south.

*Misyaar.* A marriage of convenience condoned by the Muslim religion and normally found in the Arabian Peninsula. In this marriage, the husband (who may already have one to three wives) has legal responsibilities to support his wife and any children resulting from this marriage. Women who enter into this type of marriage may be divorced or widowed and are seeking financial support for their children.

**Morality Police *(Mutawwa).*** Self-appointed enforcers of the Islamic moral code who roam the streets in Saudi Arabian cities looking for violators of the Islamic moral codes of dress and conduct. Morality police are also found in other Muslim countries, such as Iran, but are known by different local names.

**Mossad.** Israel's foreign intelligence agency, counterpart to the CIA of the United States.

**Muammar al-Qadhafi.** Libyan dictator and ruler.

*Mu'azzin.* The Muslim who calls the faithful to prayer from the minaret.

**Muhammad.** Sometimes spelled Mohammad, Mohammed, or Mohamed. Muhammad was born in 570 A.D. in the Arabian Peninsular city of Makkah and died in 632 A.D. In his late forties he claimed to be visited by the Angel Gabriel who dictated to him and demanded that he recite the new and final revelation of God to mankind.

*Munkar.* That which is forbidden by Islam, such as alcohol and pork.

*Mut'ah.* A relatively recent "designer" marriage, condoned by Islam, normally found in the Arabian Peninsula, purely for the pleasure of the two parties involved. The woman in this arrangement has no legal rights to her husband's wealth or name.

**Palestine.** The Middle East region located on the eastern Mediterranean shore bounded by Lebanon and Syria to the north, Jordan to the east, the Red Sea to the south, and the Sinai Peninsula to the southwest. Originally known to encompass the general area of Canaan and Philistia, and Moab, later named Palestina (Palestine) by the Romans. In modern times, the region of Palestine was a former Ottoman Turkish province, largely inhabited by an Arabized people and contested by Arabs and Jews. The state of Israel was carved out of a portion of Palestine by the United Nations in 1948.

**Pan Arab.** Encompassing the Arab world. Often viewed by Arab scholars as being a mythical concept because Arabs rarely agree as a group on all issues.

**Pervez Musharraf.** The first appointed president of Afghanistan following the fall of the Taliban rule in 2002.

*Qur'an.* The Muslim holy book (sometimes spelled Koran). The *Qur'an* is claimed by Muslims to be the infallible word of God as dictated to the Muslim Prophet Muhammad by the Angel Gabriel. The *Qur'an* is not to be questioned, translated, or interpreted, as that would be a corruption and distortion of the original.

**Quraish.** The tribe into which the Prophet Muhammad was born.

**Ramadan.** The holy month designated for fasting in the Muslim religion.

**Ramadan War.** The 1973 Arab-Israeli war which involved Egypt, Syria, and Israel. Also known as the Yom Kippur War.

*Reconquista.* The deliberate undoing of all Islamic and/or Arab influences by Spain and Spanish Christians following centuries of Arab occupation and rule in the Iberian Peninsula, which the Arab Muslims called *al-Andalous,* or *al-Andalousiyyah.* Hence *el Reconquista* or "The Reconquest."

**Seal of the Prophets.** The designation by Muslims given to their Prophet Muhammad as being the last of God's prophets to mankind; hence "seal."

**Shame Based Culture.** A culture which controls conformity to its values and norms through shame.

**Sheikh.** The traditional Arab family/clan/tribal leader. The position is usually acquired in a father-to-son succession, not too unlike the Native American tribal chief.

**Sykes-Picot Agreement.** The 1916 agreement between the British government representative Mr. Sykes and the French government representative Mr. Picot to divide the Middle East into two spheres of British and French influence under mandate rule once the Ottoman Turks were defeated.

**TCN (Third Country National).** Designation normally given to unskilled and blue-collar foreign guest workers. The term is also used to identify employees in a foreign embassy who are not of the embassy staff's nationality nor that of the country where the embassy is located.

**Tanakh.** The Hebrew sacred Scripture (Old Testament). Sometimes referred to as the *Torah,* although the *Torah* is considered to be technically only the first five books of the Old Testament, also known as the Pentateuch.

***Umm*** or ***Imm***. Arabic for mother. In construct, a social title to designate a woman's oldest son or daughter, such as Umm Nabeel, mother of Nabeel.

**United Nations Partition Plan for Palestine.** The 1947 United Nations plan to partition the region of Palestine into separate Arab and Jewish states. The Jews accepted the plan and established the country of Israel, and the Arabs rejected the plan, claiming all of Palestine was Arab and never established a country as of this writing.

**Usama Bin Ladin.** Exiled Saudi Arabian multimillionaire and self-appointed head of the al Qaida anti-Western, anti-Israel terrorist organization. Bin Ladin was implicated in the September 11, 2001, airline hijacking terrorist attacks on the World Trade Center in New York City, the Pentagon in Washington, D.C., and the thwarted attempt by a fourth aircraft which crashed in a Pennsylvania field.

***Waseet***. See *Wasta*. One who assumes the role of a *Wasta* and acts as an agent, broker, intercessor, intermediary, or mediator.

***Wasta***. The Arab cultural institution of agent, broker, intercessor, intermediary, or mediator. One who acts as a middle-man between two parties to affect a settlement or contract or to arbitrate a dispute.

**Yathrib.** The city in southwestern Saudi Arabia to which the Prophet Muhammad fled after being exiled from the city of Makkah. The city was later renamed by Muhammad's Muslim followers as *Madinat al-Nabi* (City of the Prophet) and later shortened to Madinah (meaning "city").

**Yom Kippur War.** The 1973 Arab-Israeli war which involved Egypt, Syria, and Israel. Also known as the *Ramadan* War.

**Zionism.** The nationalist/religious movement to reconstitute the Jewish people in their ancestral homeland in Palestine.

# Bibliography and References

## I. BOOKS

Fisher, Sydney N. 1960. *The Middle East: A History.* New York: Knopf.

Goldschmidt, Jr., Arthur. 1983. *A Concise History of the Middle East.* Boulder: Westview Press.

Held, Colbert C. 2000. *Middle East Patterns: Places, Peoples, and Politics.* Third Edition. Boulder: Westview Press.

Hitti, Philip K. 1949. *The Arabs: A Short History.* Princeton: Princeton University Press.

Hitti, Philip K. 1953. *History of the Arabs: From the Earliest Times to the Present.* Fifth Edition Revised. London: MacMillan and Co. Ltd.

*The Holy Bible. New International Version.* 1996. Grand Rapids: Zondervan.

Kaplan, Robert D. 1995. *The Arabists: A Romance of an American Elite.* New York: The Free Press.

Kirk, George E. 1945. *A Short History of the Middle East: From the Rise of Islam to Modern Times.* Washington, D.C.: Public Affairs Press.

Lewis, Bernard. 1960. *The Arabs in History.* New York: Oxford University Press.

Lewis, Bernard. 1993. *Islam and the West.* New York: Oxford University Press.

Lewis, Bernard. 1995. *The Middle East: A Brief History of the Last 2,000 Years.* New York: Scribner.

Lewis, Bernard, ed. 1976. *Islam and the Arab World.* New York: Random House.

Mansfield, Peter. 1991. *A Short History of the Middle East.* New York: Viking.

Malik, Muhammad Farooq-i-Azam. 1997. *English Translation of the Meaning of Al-Qur'an.* Houston: The Institute of Islamic Knowledge.

Millar, Fergus. 1993. *The Roman Near East, 31 B.C.-A.D. 337.* Cambridge: Harvard University Press.

O'Leary, De Lacy. 1927. *Arabia Before Muhammad.* London: Kegan Paul, Trench Trubner & Co., Ltd. New York: E. P. Dutton & Co.

Sabini, John. 1990. *Islam: A Primer.* Washington, D.C.: Middle East Editorial Associates.

Watt, W. Montgomery. 1961. *Muhammad: Prophet and Statesman.* London, New York: Oxford University Press.

## II. ARTICLES

Al-Lahiddan, Slih Bin Mohamed, Chairman of the Islamic Supreme Judicial Council of Saudi Arabia, Islamic Decree issued September 14, 2001.

Beckett, Charles A. *"Jihad."* Foundation for Advanced Study and Training (FAST), October 2001.

British Broadcasting Corp. News, Wednesday, 13, March 2002. "Q&A: UN's Palestinian State Resolution."

Nando Times Staff, "Saudi Arabia Beheads Three Men for Sodomy." *The Nando Times,* January 1, 2002.

*New York Times,* January 7, 2002. Monday, late edition-Final. "Soothing Israel's Fears."

*USA Today,* February 27, 2002. "Muslims Doubt Arabs Mounted September 11 Attack."

*Washington Post,* Sunday, February 10, 2002. "Saudi Leader's Anger Revealed Shaky Ties." Robert Kaiser and David B. Ottoway.

# Index

All foreign words are italicized. Major headings are indexed and appear in bold.

# William (Bill) Baker
## Lieutenant Colonel, United States Air Force (Ret.)

illiam (Bill) Baker was born in Pampa, Texas, in 1949. His parents moved the family to Nazareth, Israel, in 1950 where he lived and attended a local private Arab school until 1961. He spent his high school years in the Hebrew speaking regions of Israel where he continued to study Arabic and Hebrew. Professor Baker is a native Arabic and Hebrew speaker, and reads and writes both.

Following the 1967 Six-Day War, Professor Baker returned to the United States to complete high school and attend Baylor University. He was commissioned a Second Lieutenant in the United States Air Force and served twenty-seven years, retiring in 2000 as a Lieutenant Colonel. His overseas assignments included embassy tours of duty as an Assistant Air Attaché in Tel Aviv, Israel, from 1988 to 1991; acting Air Attaché in Riyadh, Saudi Arabia, from 1996 to 1997; and Defense and Air Attaché in Doha, Qatar, from 1997 to 2000. Professor Baker has worked and traveled extensively throughout the Middle East and North Africa.

Professor Baker has a Bachelor's degree in Foreign Service from Baylor University, and a Master's degree in Political Science from Southwest Texas State University. He is a graduate of the Armed Forces Joint Air Intelligence School, Air

Force Squadron's Officers School, Air Command and Staff College, Armed Forces Staff College, and the Joint Military Attaché School. As a Political-Military Affairs Officer, Professor Baker has served as Senior Middle East Intelligence Analyst at the Pentagon, Adjunct Lecturer in International Affairs at the Air Force Special Operations School, Assistant Professor of Arabic at the United States Air Force Academy, and has taught seminars on contemporary Middle East wars, the Arab culture, and Middle East history. He is currently a lecturer in Arabic and Middle East Studies at Baylor University in Waco, Texas.